MW00613472

Perfect
PAIN

This book is a memoir and sold with the understanding that the publisher and author are not engaged in rendering any services or medical opinions. The information in this book is designed to share an experience. If you suspect you have a problem that may require professional treatment or advice, you should seek competent help.

Published by PP Content, LLC
Copyright ©2018 Parham Parastaran
www.PerfectPain.com
All rights reserved.

No part of this book may be reproduced, stored in a retrieval system, or transmitted by any means, electronic, mechanical, photocopying, recording, or otherwise, without written permission from the copyright holder. To get permission for authorized use, contact book@perfectpain.com.

Cover and text design by Sheila Parr
Cover images © Konstantin Faraktinov / Shutterstock

Cataloging-in-Publication data is available.

Print ISBN: 978-0-9997739-0-1

Printed in the United States of America

First Edition

Perfect
PAIN

PARHAM PARASTARAN

PP CONTENT

To my lovely wife Jen, you are the wind beneath my wings.

Preface

I'm not a professional writer. In fact, this is my first book. I am, however, a real person with a real story. I'm not famous, and I've also never reached great heights of success as have many who write books telling their story. I named the book before I even put pen to paper to share a message that I felt many could relate to. It was the message that drove writing this book and not the stories. However, I had to tell enough stories to help deliver the message. Maybe I'll write a second book that depicts the stories I left out that may have been more interesting and more crazy. I left some detail and some stories out because I didn't want a book of stories that distract from the message . . .

Some of our greatest heroes are products of deep pain: the kind of pain that you and I can't relate to, but can only admire from afar. The kind of pain that we can't understand but can easily appreciate. Pain and suffering have inspired, motivated, and ultimately produced greatness that has transcended our world. These people have used their suffering, in most cases unknowingly, to accomplish great feats. The people I'm talking about have changed the world. You know who they are. I'm talking about the Gandhis of the world. The Jackie Robinsons of the world. The heroes that just retuned from battle. They changed the world!

My story won't the change the world. It's story about ordinary pain. Maybe just the perfect amount of pain.

My story is a true story about a regular guy living an ordinary life, with a story that might at minimum, intrigue you, and, at best, inspire you!

I've seen some dark days, but. . . .

Perfect
PAIN

PROLOGUE

Help!

Not again. *Can't stop now! I've gone too far, too far again. No turning back.* My heart is pounding out a violent rhythm. Feels as if it's about to burst out of my chest like in the cartoons I watched as kid. I'm staring at the bathroom door. Trying to not to make a single movement. I know someone is on the other side, waiting, listening. I can picture them assembling and preparing to enter. They're gonna break in. Today is the day. I'm sure of it. I briefly feel reassured as I focus on my Scotty Cameron putter and the linen cabinet that are firmly jammed between the sink and the door.

The floor is covered with magazines and cigarette butts. It's disgusting. I peer down at my hands and notice them shaking uncontrollably. I can't control my hands, and it scares me. I'm terrified. I can't be seen like this. *This is crazy,* I tell myself. *I'm crazy,* I tell myself. I check the door again, then again, making sure it is well fortified. I repeat this routine over and over. I've been preparing for this day for six years. Over time I have built better and stronger defenses, yet I've never felt fully prepared, ready.

An hour passes. Nothing. I continue to stare at the door with laser focus. I'm sure it's going to open any minute. In fact, I see it opening ever so slightly. It's been opening gradually for hours, and yet it's not opening. Why isn't it opening? I know someone is there. I can hear them organizing. I can hear everything; every sound is amplified. It's like I'm Superman or wearing a hearing aid. I even stop myself from breathing for minutes at a time so I can hear better. I need complete silence so I can hear everything: What they are saying? What they are doing? I have to know if they are coming.

Finally, I see the knob turn ever so slowly. This is it. This is real. I know what they want. They want to surprise me. Catch me in the act. Catch me off guard. I hold my breath and wait. As quietly as possible I grab all the magazines and throw them under the sink. I beg and plead with my heart and lungs to stop working so hard, to slow down. They don't cooperate. They are making too much noise.

I look back at the door; the knob is still turning, but ever so slowly. I wait patiently. Nothing? Another hour passes and still nothing. What happened? Am I seeing things? I know I saw that knob move! I need a new plan. I decide to put a mark on the door. I take my lighter and etch a line between the door and the frame. I stare at that mark for hours. If those two marks separate, I'll know for sure that the door is opening, and I'll have time to react.

React *how?* What *would* I do if they came in? I'm trapped. There is only one way out—the door. Where do I go? Where do I hide? What will I say?

Twelve hours pass and I'm still in the bathroom. Every limb

is shaking. I am squinting repeatedly, trying to get my vision in focus. I look at the faucet: I see one—then two. I blink and see it moving. I can barely hold a cigarette properly in my mouth. But I know I've got to come out soon. What do I tell her? I fell asleep? I'm sick?

Here I go! *Just open the damn door,* I tell myself. I can't quite tell if I'm hallucinating or just tired. I notice the bottle of Scotch next to a torn piece of plastic Baggie. Both completely empty. A sad thought drifts through my mind . . . then I refocus. *Separate the mark on the doorjamb from the one on the door,* I tell myself. *That's all you have to do to get out.* I hide the bottle under the sink. Then the hardest part . . . I have to flush a pack full of cigarette butts down the toilet. I avoided flushing all night because of the noise the toilet would make. But I know that I really need to get out of here. My hands and face are as white as a ghost, my mouth as dry as an Arabian desert. I need to get out of here.

My mind is starting to align with reality. I need to get the fuck out of here and can't make any noise doing it. If I don't make any noise she won't know how long I've been in here. She can't know how long I've been in here. I need to get out and go straight to the couch. She'll just think it was another long movie night—another Man Night in my Man Cave! I'll just say I got drunk and fell asleep.

I begin the risky escape. Before I open the door, I kneel down and put my head on the floor. I look through that little space between the door and the tiled floor. I'm looking for movement and a change in lighting. I'm listening for noise. And I'm praying for the best.

I've been doing this for years . . . Every time it's the same. Rituals have been part of my life since I can remember. They've evolved over the years, becoming more complex and more elaborate with time. I didn't even realize this until I met Jeckel. He was the first person to point this out to me. He educated me on how I created these rituals as a young child. But, most importantly, he eventually taught me *why* I created these rituals. Fifteen years ago I was spending an hour in the bathroom, smoking weed and looking at porn. Now I was spending an entire day in the bathroom, rolling up twenties and staring at the bathroom door.

I don't know how I got away with it for so long. I had a family, friends—people who loved me. I needed help, and I was running out of time. I was living a life resembling a grenade with the safety halfway pulled. You can live a lie only for so long. You can live life on a self-destructive path only for so long before everything crumbles. At some point you will be in a place where there is nothing left to repair. Where there is no place to hide.

I remember like it was yesterday my best friend, Andy, saying something to me that I will never forget.

"I'm not strong enough . . . I won't be able to handle it." His voice cracked, he couldn't meet my eyes. In twenty years of friendship, I had never heard him say anything like that or use that tone of voice.

"What are you talking about? Handle what?" I asked.

"The news of your death!"

CHAPTER 1

Lucky Guy!

When we bought it, I remember touching the bricks on the outside. It was all mine. I could hardly believe it.

One of the selling points of the house was the basement. It was huge, about three thousand square feet. And I had plans for it as soon as I saw it. It was my favorite part of the house, and I spent months getting every detail right as I remodeled it into the ultimate playroom for my friends and me.

I loved the entrance to the Man Room: a long, red carpet lined the hallway going to the lounge. The furniture was all custom order, picked out by our decorator: leather chairs and a very cool, specially designed couch. There was a second, separate entry: a staircase that led to the garage. Very convenient for Guys' Night because it meant no one had to come or go through the house.

The crown jewel of the Man Room suite was the poker and cigar room with its twenty-five-foot high ceiling windows at the top, and a special ventilation system so we wouldn't choke on the smoke. In the middle of the room lay a beautiful poker table with special engravings of the nicknames of the regulars who showed up every Monday night. A huge plasma TV hung over the table.

The lounge looked like some sort of shrine to Scarface: I had collected a wall of action figures and hand-drawn portraits of Al Pacino in that role, all exquisitely framed. My favorite action figure was a six-inch version of Scarface holding a wad of cash in one hand and a machine gun in the other, which I displayed in a custom, square glass case. Was I obsessed with him? Yes, I was! Like me, he was an immigrant who came from nothing and was driven by success and fitting in. As with me, he had a beautiful home and a beautiful, blonde wife. Anything to prove he wasn't that dirty and damaged kid from Cuba anymore. Like me, cocaine was part of his story as was grandiosity.

When people say they love Scarface, they focus on his excesses—the women, the piles of cocaine, and the glittering gold—or how powerful he was. The scene where he's sitting in a giant, sunken golden tub surrounded by carpet, gilded mirrors, and crystal chandeliers is one of my favorites. He's smoking a cigar and barking out orders to his best friend and wife. He's a man on the edge, but it was easy for people to be distracted by everything he had and his "the world is mine" attitude. When I watched that scene in his bathroom fit for a king, I saw the beautiful room and the cigar and the model wife, but mostly I saw a man surrounded by people who were sick of him.

That's why this one particular portrait of Scarface was my favorite. In it his shirt is half unbuttoned, his gold chains protruding from his chest. He has a pile of cocaine sitting in front of him, a glass of scotch in his hand, and a Cuban in his mouth.

The reason this portrait spoke to me, though, was the look in his eyes. I identified with that look and what it was saying. It was the story of a man who was in the process of getting everything he wanted, but he was deeply lonely, sad, and empty.

My new house, my businesses, my beautiful blonde wife . . . My home was the biggest and best out of all my friends' houses. I was thirty and living in a palace compared to the tiny apartments I had lived in just fifteen years earlier. It seemed like I was getting all the things I wanted. But I was Scarface. Deeply lonely, sad, and empty.

I remember sitting in my new basement with my buddy Jason. He and I went through a phase where all we did was smoke expensive cigars, drink expensive Scotch, and eat expensive steaks. We thought we were big shots.

This particular night was a Cuban cigar night, and I was on my sixth glass of Scotch. Jason called me "Parham-a-lot" as my close friends did. I had grand appetites for everything—fun, friends, booze, and laughter. He could never wrap his brain around why I consumed everything in such mass quantities, why I took everything to extremes. Maybe it worried him. But it always made him laugh, and to me that was more important than what I did to my body. Making my friends laugh felt good, even if it was at my expense.

The conversation turned serious. The focus drifted, like it sometimes did, to my issues. He lovingly asked, "How can you possibly have depression? I've never seen you unhappy." He gestured around the room. "You have everything. Everyone loves you! You're the most popular guy I know."

I don't remember how I answered that. But I remember

what I did. I turned and looked at Scarface staring at us from the opposite wall. And then I fixated on the piles of cocaine around him. Jason didn't understand. He was a great friend, but he wasn't a psychology guy. He thought you have to look depressed to have depression. He couldn't be further from the truth, and I didn't feel like explaining the nuances of depression to him.

So, I quickly changed the subject. I knew Jason wouldn't get it. And, frankly, I didn't really get it at the time. Jason seemed right, though. I was successful, on my way up. I was popular. I seemingly had everything, including serious depression.

The Man Room suite had two uses. One was party time with my guy friends, watching football, playing cards, or just getting drunk. The other use of the room was much darker . . . me spending hours in there with every door locked and a bottle of Scotch and as many drugs as I could get my hands on. It's where time stood still and where my soul would disappear.

Often, I would just stare at the door that led down from the garage. Like a record, over and over, I would imagine my best friends, Brian or Andy, unlocking the door and barging in on me. Finding me in that state would have been disturbing to even my closest friends, on top of the fact that they'd ruin my buzz and interfere with my desire to disconnect with the world and my hatred for myself.

My wife was terrified of coming down to my Man Cave. Even I was terrified of going down there. Heading down those stairs into my lavish playroom would trigger a physical reaction and a rapid change in my heart rate. I felt like a man going into battle knowing he might not make it out. To this day when I think about it, I get sick to my stomach, knowing that every time I went down those stairs and locked the doors could have been my death march.

My existence was exhausting, but I was well liked. That was the most important thing to me. I based my entire self-worth on the magnitude of my popularity. It was the only thing I liked about myself. As sad it was, being well liked was why I considered myself one of the "luckiest" people in the whole world. It took me a long time to figure out why that mattered so much to me.

CHAPTER 2

My First Big Move in America

I will never forget that Friday. Even now, I replay the memory of that day and that time in my life often in my mind. Sometimes just a song from the eighties is enough to trigger bittersweet memories.

It was October 1985. It was game day. I was a freshman at a high school in a northern Metro Chicago suburb. I was on the football team and played quarterback. I loved game day. Like the other players, I was strutting around the school wearing my football jersey, proudly showing off the number forty-one. I'd spent hours in the garage, acting out my favorite plays from our playbook over and over. I even remember the weather. It was sunny, not a cloud in the sky. An absolutely gorgeous fall day. A perfect day for football.

That day I also concealed a huge secret. I kept it to myself all day, but I knew I needed to tell Tony. He was my best friend, a vital person in my life. After so much instability, he was the person who was by my side every single day that I lived in Gurnee, Illinois. Every single day! I was so lucky to have him in my life.

We connected on so many levels, including the fact that his father was from Iran (his mom was American). We lived in the same neighborhood and were nearly inseparable.

I didn't know how or when to tell him my secret. I thought maybe if I didn't tell anyone, it would just go away. Maybe it wouldn't be real.

That morning my parents had told me, "We are moving tomorrow." I had zero notice that we were moving that Saturday. I don't remember my reaction. I don't remember if I said anything. I only remember how I felt. I remember the numbness I felt. I remember the anger I felt. I was in a state of shock. How could this be?

Even though we had lived in six different homes in five years, this stint in North Chicago was the longest I'd lived anywhere in my life. It was home. I had just started high school. I had a great group of friends. I was creating the family that I didn't have with these friends. They were my extended family, because I had none in America. I actually enjoyed going to school for once.

That day when I found out we were moving, my parents told me as if it were a reminder. A fucking reminder! As if they had actually discussed this like normal people would do with their children before a profound life change. Not them—that's not how they operated.

The move was news to me. Maybe I blocked it out . . . or maybe, like with most things in my life, they hadn't asked because they had discounted my feelings or need for preparation. And, as usual, they spared me the details of what to expect regarding my future.

I walked around school that day floating in disbelief. I was like the walking dead. We were moving to Champaign, Illinois. What the hell was Champaign? Where was Champaign? That night would be my last football game! My last everything here. How could this be? My mind was flooded with thoughts—and that's when it hit me. I needed to tell Tony. He was the first and only best friend I'd had since coming to America just five years earlier. How was I going to tell him? He was going to be devastated.

Looking back, this last-minute bomb being dropped by my parents was not unusual. None of it was unusual. A sudden move—I had experienced this before. A dramatic life upheaval—this was a pattern I was very familiar with. This was my parents' style, their modus operandi. I am certain these changes were tough for them as well. I'm sure they felt that it would be less painful this way. They meant no harm. It was just how they operated. Much like with the goats.

I have permanent and disturbing memories of the goats that were slaughtered in our backyard in Iran, where we had lived when I was a boy. I hated to watch. The executioner would play with the goats like it was recess. Then, bam! Their throats were slit. It happened so fast.

Supposedly the goats felt nothing. They didn't have time to be scared. They didn't have time to realize what was about to happen. They were alive one moment and dead the next. I often thought about those goats. I really hoped that they felt nothing. I hated seeing that. Now I was the goat.

Maybe my parents thought it would hurt less by waiting until the last minute. This way I wouldn't know what hit me.

No time to feel the anxiety of yet another freaking move! No time to ponder, once again, another sudden change. I didn't have any time or opportunity to fear the future. They meant no ill. I truly believe this. And they truly believed, in their minds, that this was the best thing for me. So once again, everything changed at a moment's notice.

We won the football game. All that time I'd spent practicing had paid off. But the win barely registered for me.

We had a high school dance after the game. Normally, dances were my favorite school function. Not tonight. Tonight I was attending my own funeral. I walked gingerly into the gym with Tony at my side.

The gym was half lit. Balloons and streamers were everywhere. The music was typical of a high school dance: upbeat dance songs mixed with slow love songs. Like most of the guys, I used to get anxious when a slow song came on, because we were either standing in a huddle like a bunch of losers, or, if we were lucky, we would be dancing with a girl.

But tonight, the thought of getting rejected by a girl was the least of my concerns. In fact, it seemed so silly. The fear of asking a girl to dance and being rejected that night was overshadowed by the news that my "stop" here was over.

I didn't hear a single happy song that night. I must have reworked every song to fit my mood. Tonight I only heard heartbreak.

Music was a huge part of my life. For as long as I could remember, songs served as a bookmark. Not just bookmarking periods of my life, but the feelings that went with those periods. I used music to sooth me. Lyrics were what I heard first. It was the words and what those words made me feel that mattered most to me. I am certain that at that age I listened to music differently than the other kids did.

That night I had one song playing over and over in my head. It was by one of my favorite bands of all time, a British band called Ultravox. The song was called "Dancing with Tears in My Eyes." The song didn't have the killer beat or unique riffs that most kids gravitated to. It was the words.

Dancing with tears in my eyes
Weeping for the memory of a life gone by
Dancing with tears in my eyes
Living out a memory of a love that died
It's five and I'm driving home again
It's hard to believe that it's my last time
The man on the wireless cries again
"It's over, it's over."

Everyone had heard the news about my move, and unfortunately it changed the mood of the dance. A lot of people were crying.. I had learned to "fake it till you make it" a long time ago. I was hurting as much as Tony and the others were, but I was able to hold it in like a pro. I had this overwhelming need to provide strength for my friends, especially Tony. I assured everyone that it would be okay. We would remain friends forever, as close as we were now.

But Tony wasn't buying it. His sadness made it hard to be

positive, to pretend that it was all okay. His grief over losing the friendship, me, was the most love I have ever felt. He said very little to me that night. He just held onto me. I couldn't believe this many people cared. And having them care so much made the move even more painful. I should have felt like the luckiest man alive to be so loved. Yet I felt like I would lose everything the very next day.

I was slow dancing with Tammy, my best girl friend. Tall, with dark hair, she was so pretty, and she had the best smile in the world. Tammy was a lot of fun to be around. I actually had a crush on her, but she didn't like me that way. She truly cared for me as a friend, though. She held me close, her head on my shoulders. We were cheek to cheek. I could feel her tears on my face. I could even taste the salt from her tears. She never left my side. By the end of the night, I couldn't hold it back anymore. I sat with my friends and cried.

Later that night, lying in my bed, looking up at the ceiling as I often did, I vowed that I would never feel this way again. I promised myself that I would *never cry again*. Except for the following morning, I managed to keep that promise for two decades.

The experience I had that night would prove to be a central piece of the psychology of how I coped with the complicated puzzle that was my life. I realized that night that I was popular, and I realized how being popular made me feel. I realized that being popular was painful. I also realized that not being popular would be painful. Popularity was my "blanky" and pacifier.

The next day came, and my only memory of that Saturday morning was me sitting in the car outside the rental home that we were leaving behind. I was crying and my dad came up to me and asked why. I told him I was crying because I was leaving my friends. He said, "You shouldn't cry; these aren't your real friends. You're too young to have real friends. What matters most are the friends you will have when you are grown up."

Good-bye Gurnee and the best friends I had ever had.

CHAPTER 3

Painful Realization

I don't remember when I smiled again after that move to Champaign. All I can remember thinking was how much this town sucked.

The day we arrived was overcast, a gloomy fall day. Champaign was the ugliest town I'd ever seen. Everything was dirty. I hated every house I saw. I hated the doors, the roofs, and the windows on every house and building. Old and nasty. The houses were depressing to look at. Driving through town, I was disgusted by everything—even the businesses—I was seeing in this new town. It was nothing like Gurnee.

I was even more disgusted when we got to our new place. It was a very small apartment with just two bedrooms. I had already lived in several apartments since I'd been in America, but this was the first time I was angry about our "home." This move wasn't fair. How many more times was this going to happen me? Another fucking new school—my fifth in five years!

I was standing at the bus stop the following week. It was only a few hundred yards from our apartment. But this bus stop was not the same as the one in Gurnee; at that one I'd met Tony. This stop was on a main road instead of being in a neighborhood. At my last school, I rode a regular yellow school bus. This town apparently didn't have those. I had to ride a city bus, the Brown 9A.

I remember that first bus ride like it was yesterday. I walked on that bus and went straight to the back without making eye contact with anyone. I hated everyone on that bus. There were adults, college students, and maybe five kids around my age. Where were all the kids who were going to the high school?

I sat down and immediately put on my headphones. I had one of those giant-sized Walkmans. I put in my Ultravox cassette. I sat on the Brown 9A and listened to the song "Dancing with Tears in My Eyes" over and over again.

We pulled to a stop at a building that looked like a school. It was a very old building in the middle of town. It didn't have a football field or anything that resembled my old high school. *This must be my new high school,* I thought.

I watched all five kids get off the bus. I stood up and got my stuff together. Took a couple of steps forward and then stopped. Just stopped. I turned around and returned to my seat, put the music back on. I stared at the kids standing in front of the school, laughing as the bus pulled away.

Looking out the window, I tried to like something about this town. But I couldn't. The more I rode the angrier I got and the more I hated this place. I rode the Brown 9A for what seemed like hours. The battery on my Walkman ran out and so did my patience for riding that stupid bus.

I got off the bus somewhere on the college campus of the

University of Illinois, where my brother had just begun his freshman year. Interesting choice for a move! Back then the coincidence of moving to a town where my brother started college didn't even strike me.

I was lost. I walked all over that campus. I was physically lost. But nothing compared to how lost my soul was. I noticed a set of dorms that resembled my brother's. I remembered it from when we moved him here only a few months back. With a little digging I figured out where his room was and headed right up. He was shocked when he opened the door.

"What are you doing here?" he asked.

"I'm lost," I said.

"Lost? What do you mean, lost?"

"I couldn't figure out where my new school was," I told him. I told him about the big people on the bus, adults. Only a few kids. I thought I must have been on the wrong bus. "I swear!" I said. I don't know if he believed me.

My brother was nice to me that day. He wasn't always nice to me, growing up. There was a time I thought he hated me. He was especially tough on me when he was in high school. Things weren't always easy for him; life was not fair to him either. He was one of those brilliant kids with a big brain—a genius. In Iran, geniuses were admired. All my parents' friends admired him for his big brain. Here in America, I learned— and he learned—that the jocks, rich kids, and pretty ones were admired.

Some thirty years later, I found out that he was as shocked as I was that my parents showed up in Champaign. He told me he didn't know we were moving there until we actually got there and my parents called him to tell him we were living in Champaign. I was sad for him, too, then but not surprised to learn this.

I spent the rest of my first day of school with his friends and some of the guys on his floor. These guys were really nice to me. I decided that they would be my new best friends. In fact, I connected with my brother's friends and they remained my friends for a long time. Screw high school, I decided. I'm going to college!

Eventually I made my way back to the bus and headed home. I don't think I spoke to my parents when I got home. I didn't tell them about my first day *not* at school. But that wasn't unusual. We just never had much to talk about.

They both worked a lot. My mom quickly got back to work after the move. She was working at McDonald's when we left Gurnee and immediately started working at the local McDonald's in Champaign.

The next day I got up and got ready for school. Got on the Brown 9A and attempted to go to school. Again I watched a handful of kids get on the bus and get off at the high school, just like they were supposed to. But not me . . . I wasn't getting off. I *couldn't* get off. That day I decided to walk around a bit and explore the university campus again. I did the same thing the day after and the day after that. I just kept repeating this pattern.

I remember that one of those days at the university I tracked my brother down again. It was lunchtime at his dorm.

"Why aren't you going to school?" he asked.

"I will . . . tomorrow, I promise!" I said.

That was clearly a lie. I had no plans to ever attend that new high school. After a bit of scolding from my brother, I was rewarded with the best lunch I had ever had in my life. I couldn't believe that college dorms gave you so much food. I stuffed myself at the buffet. It was better than McDonald's, which was my favorite restaurant at the time. Then I listened to some music and headed home.

This routine went on for the entire week. (I didn't go see my brother anymore, though. I was worried he would tell my parents.) I just rode the bus around and walked the campus. I knew I couldn't get away with it forever; I was just delaying the inevitable. I have no idea what broke the pattern but, the next week, I got off the Brown 9A at the high school stop and finally went to school. No one was worried where I'd been. No one seemed to care.

My first real day at school sucked. I knew no one. All these kids already had friends. They had history and a bond with each other that I didn't have with them—like the bond I had had with Tony and Tammy back home. But I did make one friend that first day. His name was Freddy. He was a senior in my freshman biology class. I sat next to him. He asked what my story was, so I told him. I was new, just moved from Chicago. Then he asked me if I'd ever had a Gutbuster. It was the most popular pizza slice in town. Of course I hadn't. He even invited me to go with him to Garcia's Pizza in a Pan that day for lunch.

I didn't believe you could leave campus for lunch at this school. I was a little nervous to go with him, but it would have made me more nervous to turn down his invitation. He was a big black guy, intimidating, and a senior. I wasn't about to be a pussy on my first day of school.

Miss Freeman finally finished talking about frogs, and I was on my way to Garcia's to try a Gutbuster. Each slice of the pizza weighed ¾ of a pound, loaded down with sausage, pepperoni, mushrooms, green pepper, and onions.

Freddy seemed to like me, and I was glad. He was a big dude; he could protect me. At the same time, he made me nervous, because older guys had made me nervous ever since I was a kid. They reminded me of my cousin in Iran. He had also pretended to like me, but he proved to be a liar. So I was always on guard around older men. I never knew what they wanted. As it turned out, Freddy didn't want the same things my cousin wanted.

Freddy was the only guy I remember talking to that day. I distinctly remember realizing that, even though he was a nice guy, I didn't have any friends. I was starting over again.

CHAPTER 4

My First Big Move

Nothing stood out to me more than that train ride. It was like something out of the movies. (When I described it to Jeckel, he said it reminded him of *Doctor Zhivago*. I've never seen that movie, but I'll take his word for it.)

Parts of the roof of the train car were missing, and a lot of the windows didn't have any glass in them. There were no seats, just benches running through the middle of the car. It was basically a box with wooden floors. Packed with people—literally on top of each other, like animals—all strangers. The only people I knew were my mom and my brother. I can hardly remember a single woman besides my mom; it was mainly men, all intimidating. I was nine years old. I think I was terrified—or at least I should have been. For a long time, all I could remember were the details of the ride but nothing about how I felt.

I remember making a corner of the train my home. I was crouched down. I spent the ride staring at the floor. I didn't want to make eye contact with anyone. And if my memory serves me right, my mom did the same.

We didn't say anything. I wanted to scream, "Hey mom, what the hell is going on?" But I didn't. We've never discussed it to this day.

At one of the stops, a guard grabbed one of the other passengers, one of the men. The guy appeared to be a very, very fat man. The guard grabbed him and started ripping his clothes off. I don't know what I expected to see, but I suddenly realized the guy wasn't fat at all. He had wrapped his entire upper body with fabric and textiles. A smuggler.

I remembered noticing this guy before the guard picked him out. For some reason he looked like a Russian lacquer doll to me. He wore brightly colored clothing and his face was bright red, like he was wearing makeup. He was ridiculous, a caricature. Then all of a sudden I saw the guard beating him silly. I turned away . . . That was that.

The memory of the train ride and the smuggler was the product of a few years of therapy. I was thirty-one and seeing Jeckel twice a week. He was a psychiatrist, but he wasn't the first psychiatrist I had seen. Unlike others, he wasn't into writing prescriptions. He wasn't Doctor Feel-Good. Jeckel practiced psychoanalysis. He wanted to know *who* I was and *why* I was, questions I had never known or even wanted to ask myself.

I spent the next fifteen years, hours upon hours, in his office. At first Jeckel would hardly say anything. It would be complete silence in that little room unless I had something to say. I always sat in the chair. There was also a couch in that little room. Many patients in psychotherapy lie on the couch to allow their minds to be free. But not me. I refused to lie on a couch next to another man.

It was there, in that office, that I found my memory.

Human beings have this incredible gift of suppressing their memory to limit pain. It is our mind's defense system. For example, I have a friend who took a bad fall while hanging Christmas lights. He described in vivid detail knowing he had fallen and then seeing his leg dangle. It was broken in half. They had to put in screws to rejoin the two parts. I asked him how badly that hurt. His answer didn't surprise me. He said he couldn't feel a thing.

How was that possible? How could he snap his leg in half and feel nothing? How could I flee from Iran on a train surrounded by violence and suffering and feel nothing? I believe it is just what our mind does to protect us.

The human mind has an amazing capability of suppressing pain. In my friend's case it was physical pain. Without that intervention, his pain would have been unbearable. The same philosophy applies to our psychological well-being. Our mind protects us, in the short run, from the unbearable mental pain we face, from our psychological snapped legs.

I lost a great deal of my early childhood to this phenomenon. Not like someone who has amnesia—I remember the actual events. I just don't remember the pain. I don't remember the fear. My feelings were numbed. I would compare it to being anesthetized before having your teeth drilled by a dentist. You see his hands holding a drill and rudely putting it in your mouth. You can even clearly hear the annoying buzz of the drill. Yet you feel nothing.

After a few years of therapy, I realized what Jeckel was doing. He wanted me to unlock the feelings associated with the events of my past. More specifically, he wanted me to feel what the child in me had felt. Not through my adult lens, decades later. That lens sees the world differently. For the most part that adult lens is guarded and logical.

He wanted me to feel how the scared little boy in me experienced these events. And I learned that it was this scared little boy's experiences that shaped the craziness that was living inside my head, the genesis of the depression I suffered. The craziness that drove me to create "fixes" like the need to be social and popular, my insatiable appetite for cigars and steaks and nice houses, and, of course, my desire to lose myself in drugs.

It took a long time to assemble the pieces, but little by little my memories leaked out like a slow drip in a sink.

Most of the almost-four years we lived in Iran were seemingly stable. My parents and my brother and I lived there from when I was five until I was nine years old. My dad, an American-educated engineer, was the head honcho of a pretty big factory in Isfahan, one of the biggest cities in Iran. It's also where I was born, so I suppose, technically, this was my second time living in Iran. We had left Iran when I was one year old to come to America while my dad went to college.

We lived about twenty minutes or so outside of Isfahan in a small village called Baghambrisham. My memories are really limited to the last two years of our time there when I was between seven and nine years old.

Baghambrisham was a village of the kind you see on a National Geographic special. Dirt roads, dust, and people living in very small spaces. For example, a lot of the villagers used animals as their main source of transportation. People did their laundry in the river that ran through the village. I remember clothes hanging to dry on lines from all the houses.

Many of the villagers in Baghambrisham worked in the factory where my father was president. Their houses were tiny and constructed out of mud. We were privileged, however. My family lived in a compound, a giant house. Our entire home was guarded by tall walls that served as the perimeter of the compound. We had a large pool and a garden, and there weren't any houses around us. Still, dirt roads led to our front gates.

The best part of the house was the view from that entrance. The compound opened directly onto a small mountain range. Looking back, I can see why so many Iranians fled to California after the revolution. So much of Iran resembles the landscape surrounding LA: big cities flanked by big mountains, mild weather. From our house I could see the top of the mountain we lived closest to. I used to play in those mountains all the time with my brother. We were always playing outside. Always playing.

When we weren't playing, we were in school. We didn't attend the local school. The school in the village was in a little dirt building and all the kids wore sandals. Me, I wore shoes. My brother and I also wore uniforms. My uniform was a white-and-blue striped shirt and blue pants. We had a version with shorts and a version with pants. I believe the kids that went to this school were different from the kids that went to the school in the village. These kids' parents were doctors, engineers, and professors.

Our school was in Isfahan and it was part of the university campus. I can't tell you anything about the classes except that we also studied English and that I played soccer every day at school. I remember the soccer. I was playing soccer every chance I had. I was pretty good! I was always the first or second kid chosen when we picked teams—one of the best in my school.

I played outside school too. (When I wasn't playing soccer, I was playing soccer.) I think that is what all the Iranian kids did. Playing on grass fields was not a requirement. We played in the street, whether it was asphalt or dirt. The nicest field we played on was a big grass field at our school where we used real soccer balls. Otherwise, we all used these plastic soccer balls that I have never seen again since leaving Iran. As long as I was playing soccer, nothing mattered. I was crazy for it.

In Iran I also loved to tell jokes. I must have been good at telling them, because my parents always had me perform these comedy acts at their dinner parties. I knew so many jokes that I had a whole stand-up routine. My mom, especially, was proud of having a charming, cute boy who entertained friends and family at gatherings. I think I may have even liked it at the time. Today, I can't remember a joke I heard three minutes earlier.

My life was seemingly very normal in Iran until it wasn't.

I came home one day after school to a strange scene. My mom was frantic. She was talking to me but looking through me. I had never seen her like this. My dad was nowhere to be found.

Awkwardly, I tried to ask her what was happening, but her answers made no sense. She was packing. Barely looking at me. I was so confused. I was nine at the time.

I asked a couple more questions, like, "Where is Dad?" and "When will we see him?" I don't remember any answers. It is even possible I never asked those questions and just thought them in my head. My memory is hazy.

I stopped asking questions, I think. I went into my room and waited.

Finally, unable to bear it anymore, I asked again, "Why didn't Dad wait for us? Is everything okay?"

"Nothing is wrong!" she said, sadly.

I stopped talking. I stopped asking. I started crying.

Next thing I knew, my mom, my brother, and I were in Tehran at my aunt's apartment, one of my favorite places to be. While it wasn't unusual for us to drive the eight hours to go visit my aunt, these circumstances seemed strange. My aunt was always nice to me. This time, she was being especially nice. But she wasn't talking either.

That night I went on the roof to hang out as we often did when visiting her. Not a cloud in the sky. I saw something I had never seen. There were jet fighters in the sky putting on a show like no other. Red streaks of light covered the entire horizon.

From the roof it just looked like roman candles illuminating the sky as the fighter jets maneuvered around the streaks. There was one fire after another, right above me, in the sky. The entire sky was lit up. I couldn't take my eyes off of this show.

"What's going on, brother?" I asked.

"We're at war," my brother explained.

"Who's at war?"

"We are."

"Why?" I asked my brother.

"Because Saddam Hussein doesn't like us!"

This is the only explanation I remember, although I am sure

my brother provided a much more intelligent answer than that. I was only nine, so this is what my memory has reduced it to. My brother was so smart that I didn't understand what he said anyway, most of the time.

Before we went to bed that night, my brother also told me that we were flying to another country in a couple of days to join my dad. Finally I had an answer, or part of an answer. I do remember that I missed my dad.

Two days came and went and no plane ride.

We were now driving in a car packed with our luggage. It was cramped in that car with the three of us along with all the bags and boxes we had brought. The driver didn't say a word.

Where is he taking us? Why is it taking so long? I want to get out of here now! I want to see my dad. I don't remember asking any questions out loud. Only in my head. I had learned to keep my mouth shut. No point in asking. No one explained things to me anyway. So that's what I did. I looked out the window and minded my own business.

Finally the car stopped. We were definitely not in Tehran anymore. We were in some small village outside the big city. We got out of the car. My mom talked to someone I didn't know, we were loaded into a new car, and we were off again.

Another car ride! A shorter one this time but even more cramped. Again we stopped to talk to someone. Walked into someone's office, exchanged a few words, and climbed into another car.

My memories of this aren't clear. Just a whirlwind of car rides punctuated by conversations with people I had never met and never seen. I had no idea where we were going or what we were doing. All I could think about was that my dad was not here and there wasn't going to be any plane.

At long last we arrived at what seemed to be the final destination. No car was waiting for us. A man told my mom to follow him. We followed him without any question. We were doing what everyone told us to do. Why was my mom so accommodating? She must have known what she was doing.

I couldn't help thinking that I hadn't played soccer in a few days. I really missed playing soccer. I wondered when I would play again . . .

Sadly, I never touched a soccer ball again. Not in Iran, and not in the United States.

We were dropped off at a train station—what seemed like a very busy one. I remember people everywhere; the train station was dirty and full of dirty people. I didn't see very many kids. I remember thinking that I preferred the airport to this scary train station. Why couldn't we have just taken a plane like my mom said? Eventually I began to understand the plan. This was how we were going to get to out of Iran. I would see my dad soon.

Later I learned what was going on. Iran was in the midst of an Islamic revolution. The Iranian king had been ousted and a new leader had emerged. This new regime was Islamic and we weren't Muslim, so we had to go.

In fact, a few weeks prior to all this, a group of workers at the factory rebelled against my dad because of our religion. We were also privileged, while they were poor, which may have had something to do with it.

These people stormed my father's office. They were prepared

to hurt him, maybe even kill him. My dad doesn't remember anything except giving a compelling speech to hold them off for the moment. He doesn't even remember what he said, but it was enough to convince them to spare his life.

What I do know for sure is that he came home and immediately got the hell out of Iran. Apparently he thought he was in more danger than we were. We would be okay on our own for a few days, which would also allow my mom to tidy up our affairs.

Ultimately the plan was for my mom to get our finances in order and gather our valuables and then to fly to Pakistan to join my father. Then, we would get political asylum from the U.S. government. We would start a new life in America. The entire plan went awry once the Tehran airport was bombed by Iraq in the war that was simultaneously happening.

Once the airport was bombed, my father used his connections to design a plan to get us out of Iran through a complicated series of transportation connections that culminated in the train ride to Karachi, Pakistan. All we were able to bring was some clothes.

The train moved very slowly. We started somewhere in the desert and rode through the night. No food, no water, no sleep. The desert gets very cold at night, and I froze my ass off. What kind of train operated with missing parts and no windows?

Once in a while the train would stop. It was at one of these stops that the guards grabbed the fat man I described earlier and beat him badly, ripped the textiles off his body, and took him away. All this happened ten feet in front of me. I stayed as quiet as I could be. I wished I were invisible. I was so scared that it was like all my emotions were just turned off.

For decades when I thought of this I could never remember feeling afraid. I just remember being quiet, like the whole thing had happened to someone else and I was just watching a movie of it.

Of all the parts of this story—me a nine-year-old boy with my mom and brother trying to escape from Iran in a train that was not a train—I think about the fat man all the time. I can never forget him. I felt sorry for that man. The stress and pain on his face are burned in my memory.

We somehow endured that awful night on the train. I was literally starving the entire time. I was a boy who loved to eat!

After the whole night had passed I thought we must have been getting close to our final stop. The train had fewer people on it than when we started. I noticed a man prying up and disassembling the train's wooden floors. As the floor opened up, he grabbed a bunch of boxes and started throwing them off the train. He wasn't the only one doing this. The floor was coming apart to reveal mystery boxes that had been buried and hidden in the floor. One by one they were tossed out of the train. Again, I was a good observer but didn't ask any questions and didn't receive any explanations.

Later, I figured out that the reason there were no kids on this train was because it wasn't the kind of train that people used to travel on vacations or see family. This was a train for smugglers or the kind of people who can't buy tickets on normal trains. That's why guards kept coming on the train. That's why the train made so many strange stops.

We arrived somewhere in Pakistan. My mom, brother, and I grabbed our belongings and left the train. I still didn't know what was happening, but I was so relieved to be off the train that I felt things could only get better. I felt like I could breathe again after holding my breath for twenty-four hours.

I was sure we had been on that train for three days but it was only twenty-four hours. The worst was behind us. And finally food! I remember eating the spiciest eggs I had ever eaten in my life and being so grateful for them. It was the first real meal I had in a long time.

Once in Pakistan, we were reunited with my dad. A few days later we were granted political asylum by the American government. I am sure it was much more complicated than this, but to a nine-year-old the end result was all that mattered.

CHAPTER 5

Welcome to California

One of the first things I remember about getting to California was hearing this one particular song on the radio. It was called "Do the Hustle." To me, that song felt so American. It felt so white. It felt so rich. It felt so cool. It felt so clean and foreign. And I felt so out of place. Looking around, I thought everyone was so pretty. Everyone was white, and blonde people were everywhere!

It was 1980. We had fled from Iran and officially made America our new home. We had been granted asylum and we were here to stay.

I had lived in America before, but this version of America was new to me. I had come as an infant in the early '70s while my dad attended college. We had lived in Stillwater, Oklahoma, until I was five years old. I don't have any memories of our time in Oklahoma except hearing tornado sirens weekly and watching people kill snakes. My only other memories are from looking through old photos. I think I was a happy kid then, at least from what I can see in the pictures.

Fleeing from Iran, hiding out in Pakistan, and moving

8,000 miles was about as confusing and turbulent a time as any child could go through. To make it worse, my parents did not do a lot of explaining. I had no idea what was happening, but there were too many questions to ask: Why are we here? Where are we going to live? What about our home in Baghamrisham? All the questions I had ever asked them before remained unanswered, so why bother now? Why make it harder for my parents than it already seemed to be? I kept my questions to myself and sort of just existed.

We moved into a small two-bedroom apartment in Orange County. Not the Orange County you see in reality shows with beach mansions and flashy cars. We were very poor. We literally came here with only as much as my parents could carry. Their decision to flee Iran had been sudden. My father was effectively exiled without notice. So, even if his bank account had been accessible to him (the money was frozen), he and my mother didn't have time to gather our assets and bring to America the savings they had accumulated.

Although we were poor, the America I saw around us was not. In my eyes we had gone from living in black-and-white television to high definition.

The roads! They were amazing. Clean and sharp. Not dirt like the roads back home.

I couldn't get over the highways. They were perfectly paved. The cars traveled so smoothly and quickly over them. The cars were so nice, so new and expensive-looking.

Then there were the lights. Freakin' lights everywhere! The streets, the tall buildings, the parks, and the neighborhoods all lit up like the pictures you'd see on a postcard.

And the fast food restaurants: Carl's Jr., McDonald's, and Burger King. I was obsessed with these restaurants. They served food like I had never tasted before. We didn't eat there a lot, but when we did it was a treat for me. That was how my infatuation with fast food started. It was one of my first "fixes."

I think we arrived in California in October. The weather wasn't particularly warm, and I don't remember swimming in the ocean. But I do remember my first day of school.

I walked down a hallway in my new school. I have no clue what the name of the school was, but I remember every detail of how it looked. The school was perfect. There was carpet in the hallways and the classrooms. My classroom was in a hallway by the library. I remember totally inconsequential details like how the hallway actually sloped down just before you got to my class. I was so impressed with this amazing new place.

"Kids, gather around. We have a new student." That's what my teacher said on my first day in my perfect new school. I had no clue what her name was, but she was nice. She made me feel welcome.

All the kids in the class were just staring at me. At least that's what I remember. All day in class all I could think was that the room was so nice. I remember spending lots of time on the floor doing stuff. The carpet was clean and perfect.

I made a friend in class on the first day. He was a cool guy. Blond hair and everything. I made more friends outside on the playground playing a game I had never played before. The kids bounced a red ball against a wall with their hands. I had used my legs to play soccer. Now, all of a sudden, I had to learn to use my hands. Weird. But it wasn't long until I got the feel for it.

In a few days I went from getting picked last in games to getting picked first or second. Surprisingly, I was enjoying school. Once the boys gave me a chance, they found out that I was all right. The girls were another story.

Our apartment was close to the school. I walked to and from school everyday. On the way, there was this park. I used to stop there and stare at the kids. They looked so happy. They had their friends. I would just sit somewhere and watch them. I even caught a boy and girl kissing. I wondered what it was like to have best friends like that, to have girls that wanted to kiss me. To be liked for something more than being good at sports. These were questions I would never ask my brother or my parents.

America, with its big roads and clean carpets, was amazing, but I was lonely.

I didn't talk to my parents a lot. At home, I watched TV. I would get up early and watch cartoons. I watched TV in Iran, but not like here. The number of TV channels and shows in America was overwhelming.

I became obsessed with watching shows with fighting, especially karate. I watched anything with karate in it, which explains my first neurotic behavior. I walked around in public doing karate chops and kicks. I think it bothered my parents and my brother. I remember them telling me to quit it all the time.

America was amazing, but something was wrong. My dad and mom weren't the same. I think they were at odds. There was distance between them for sure. Having your life uprooted probably had something to do with that. But I think as far as they were concerned, only their lives had been uprooted—not my brother's or mine. Why do I think this? Because no one bothered to tell me what was going on. No one bothered to ask me how I was doing. So I went to school, played at recess, tried to make friends, and kept to myself.

My memories from this time are still hazy, so I pay attention to the small details that stick out crystal-clear.

I was at school, in art class. We were allowed to draw whatever we wanted. So I started drawing, my pencils flying across the paper. When I finished, I showed my teacher. I always thought of myself as a good drawer, so I looked at her face expecting some praise.

She tried—she really tried—but the face I saw was not of a proud teacher. She was concerned, but trying to not show it. She asked me why I had drawn this. I told her I was good at drawing these types of drawings. She asked how long I had been drawing this. I told her for a long time. She took the drawing from me and walked away.

The next day my teacher told me that I was going to meet with someone in the school about something. I didn't understand, but I went to this woman's office. She introduced herself and was very nice. I noticed she had my drawing sitting on her desk.

After some small talk, she asked me about the drawing. She asked if I'd seen this thing I had drawn in Iran. I casually said, "Yes, all the time." She asked me a bunch of other questions: questions about my parents, brother, and life in general. I think she realized that my drawings were normal for a kid that had just come from Iran. What was normal for me was clearly not normal here.

That day I felt the foreigner in me. And thereafter I never drew anything but happy people and airplanes. My drawings like that first one I had done were something these people weren't used to. I had drawn a picture of people protesting in the streets, holding up signs, with helicopters flying above. The helicopters were shooting down onto the crowd. I drew people lying in the streets dead or with wounds to their chests and bleeding. To this day, I can still draw that scene perfectly on paper.

The other memory that sticks out from my time in California happened when I thought I was going to have a great day. We were going shopping. Like any fourth grader, I loved toys. I remember being at a house. I remember going through someone's toys. We were at a garage sale, I assume. I remember going through the toys in that house with a feeling of pure joy. I was so excited to play with this particular action figure, a Boba Fett toy that was a foot tall. I remember leaving with some toys.

But something changed. I had to give them back. To this day I don't know why. But, having those toys and giving them back is burned in my memory as firmly as the memory of the fat man on the train. I felt so ashamed, and I felt so helpless.

The rest of my time in California isn't so clear, but I know that school was quickly becoming my haven. I loved it. I had friends and a teacher that really liked me. I looked forward to going every day. I was happy again until . . .

"Gather around kids. I have an announcement to make," my teacher said.

We all got in a circle on the floor of that perfectly clean and nice carpet. She pulled down the map of the United States that was on a roller hanging from the chalkboard. Then she wrote something on the board: C-H-I-C-A-G-O. She pointed to something on the map and said, "This is where Parham is moving. Chicago."

I had been there only a few months and we were already moving. I don't remember my parents telling me or talking to me about it. I'll give them the benefit of the doubt that it's my problem. Perhaps I don't remember. But I do remember the shock. I do remember the feeling in my stomach. It's the same feeling I have as I write this today.

So we left the ocean and my fair-haired friends for a place that was the exact opposite of the beauty I saw when I first got to California. For the first time in my life, I would experience serious snow, and it would be cold as hell.

CHAPTER 6

Windy City

The Chalet Apartments. That was our new home, in the town of Joliet, Illinois, a forty-five-minute drive southwest of Chicago. The Windy City! My sixth city in four or five months. My third home and school in the same amount of time.

I was getting used to this constant upheaval of my life. Here's a new room, a new school, make new friends, don't complain. I wasn't mad anymore. I wasn't even really confused anymore. I didn't have any more questions—why are we moving? Where will we live? Didn't matter. My adaptation skills were improving.

In reality, I was emotionally numbed. I just existed.

Yet again, there is a lot I don't remember about this time in my life—or perhaps choose to not remember. But I do recall the song I heard as we pulled into the Chalet Apartment: "Betty Davis Eyes" by Kim Carnes. It started with this amazing synthesizer mixed with a tiny bit of hi-hat. I loved it. I think that exact moment is when my affinity for female singers and voices began. Sigmund Freud and Jeckel have a lot to say about why.

In California, everything was sunny and blond. In Joliet, everything was brown. Huge buildings of brown, ugly brick. There were maybe twenty of these hulking buildings in our complex.

Our apartment was toward the back, right next to a field. It was really small, even smaller than our apartment in California. We were in a sunken first-floor apartment that you would walk down into, meaning the windows were about level with the ground. Strange for a boy who was used to living in a home that looked out onto mountains.

Living halfway in the ground wasn't the only thing new to me. In California, I remember everyone being white. In Joliet, especially in my complex, it seemed like everyone was black or Hispanic. I fit right in! But people weren't as happy and nice as they were in California. In fact, living in Joliet was the first time I remember being scared to walk alone or be outside after dark, even after everything I'd seen in Iran.

First thing I did was get enrolled in my new school. School in California had been pretty fun once I had made friends, so I had a good attitude and expected the same. I couldn't wait to meet my teacher, my new friends, and my new life. Plus this new life had snow. I had never been around anything like this snow stuff.

My first day of school was a cold, cloudy, and just flat-out ugly day. My new teacher was nothing like the gentle, sweet woman who had taught fourth grade in California. He wasn't very nice to me, and he had a wooden leg. I soon learned that he had no problem kicking the students, even a new student, with that leg.

But I quickly made friends, and I quickly acclimated to this new environment and school. I also took one important lesson from the last school and quickly implemented it. In art class I drew one thing only: happy people playing!

It wasn't long before I had a new best friend, Todd. A little guy! He introduced me to his favorite band, Kiss. And just like that, I was a fan. Those guys were amazing, the first band I fell in love with.

Todd also loved karate as much as I did, and we used to watch Bruce Lee movies together. But I wanted more than to be a fan: I wanted *to be* Bruce Lee. So I started writing scripts. I wrote and wrote. I wasn't like most kids, starting a project with enthusiasm and then petering out because it's too much work. I wrote complete scripts of karate-themed movies that I then acted out. They all starred Bruce Lee, so I played Bruce Lee. I can still feel and remember the paper I wrote those scenes on. Paper that had been written and rewritten on many times, with eraser marks everywhere.

All my early scripts had a hero in them. The story basically went like this: I am a good guy. I get screwed and taken away from my love, a beautiful girl. I eventually go from being the helpless victim with all the odds against me to being the hero that beats the crap out of everyone and gets the girl back. What would Jeckel think of those scripts? I've never asked.

You would think having to make new friends and adjusting to an abusive teacher would be what was making my life hard, but it wasn't. School, karate, and Kiss were my escape: a little world invented by a boy who wanted to have fun and needed to distract himself from home.

Home was tough. My parents were busy trying to put food on the table. Turns out we moved to the Chalet Apartments because my dad had gotten a job there. I think he was the site manager. My dad had a real office, and we got free housing. He didn't make much money, but it was a start. I've never asked him, but I've always been curious why he didn't try to find work as an engineer. He had a degree from an American university and experience as a manager, after all.

The complex was owned by a group of people, one of whom was a good friend of my parents from before I was born. In Iran, they had been neighbors. The man got out of Iran early and had become a very successful surgeon in the Chicago area. His family lived in a beautiful house in the suburbs. They took us in and really made me feel good. I didn't have any family in the United States, so these people were all I had.

In our culture, friends of your parents whom you are very close with can be referred to as your uncle and aunt. Their kids are then your cousins, even if you aren't related by blood. This surgeon was now my uncle, his wife my aunt, and their boys my cousins. For the rest of my life. I loved and love them like family. We are still close to this day. When I see my aunt and uncle I feel pure joy, just like I am a little kid again. Back when I was a little kid, going to their house was a wonderful escape.

It wasn't long before I noticed the major contrast in our lifestyles, mine and my cousins'. I was so jealous. I wanted to be the surgeon's kid.

It makes me feel terrible for my parents to feel this way about another family. The changes that happened in my childhood weren't their fault. They had gotten screwed as well. That didn't change the fact that I wanted a different life, though, the kind of life my cousins had.

My parents made friends and connections as quickly as I did. Besides the surgeon and his family, we made new friends through the local Baha'i community. Being Baha'i was why we had to leave Iran. When the revolution happened, anyone who was a Baha'i was jailed and tortured. No one was safe, including my immediate family on my dad's side. For example, my dad's youngest sister was a devout follower, so strong in her faith that she never would have renounced it. She did not manage to escape Iran. She was jailed and tortured.

My family entrenched themselves in the Baha'i community. We went to the rundown Baha'i center in Joliet all the time. I went to classes and group events. Everyone was welcoming, especially a couple of the older guys. One was named Randy. He played the sax, which I thought was amazing. The other's name was Artist. He played guitar.

They were so much older than my brother and me, but, for twentysomethings, they spent a lot of time with us. I don't know why they were so good to us. For example, Artist took me to see the *Star Wars* movie, the coolest thing someone could have done for a kid my age—something I never experienced with my father.

Randy and Artist knew how much I liked the drums. Even when I lived in Iran, I didn't have a set, so I used to arrange my mom's pots and pans into a drum set and bang away. Those guys had a connection to a studio—with an actual drum set in it—and they took me one day. I couldn't believe it. The drums were perfect, the most beautiful thing I had ever seen or heard.

I banged on that thing and it produced the sweetest sounds. I remember trying to play along to REO Speedwagon. There was a three-cymbal sequence that I nailed. I felt so cool, and I was so grateful that I had people looking out for me like this, people who wanted to make me feel special.

Now I wanted a drum set. I remember like it was yesterday. My dad was sitting in a chair in the living room by the front door facing the TV. On his left, by his arm, was a small coffee table with a lamp on top. It was nighttime.

I asked if I could get a drum set. He looked at me, grabbed a pen, and began striking the table with the pen like it was a drumstick.

He said, "Do you hear that?

"No," I said.

Then he tapped the table again with his pen and asked the same question. "Do you hear that?"

Frustrated I said, "Hear what? The pen hitting the table? Yeah, but so what? What does this have to do with getting a drum set"?

He explained that every time he struck a different part of the table it made a different sound. I didn't know what to say. Then he said, "Do you know how hard it is to play drums?"

He wasn't really asking.

So that was that. Either we didn't have any money to buy a drum set, or he really thought I was not capable of becoming a drummer. I am guessing it was the former. With as much pride as he had, it was probably too difficult to say we couldn't afford drums.

A whole year passed, our longest stretch in one town for

some time. I started fifth grade. We kept going to the Baha'i center. My dad was doing well at work. I even got that starter drum set, and my brother got an organ.

We played music all the time. We were addicted. We had a little radio with a tape recorder. We couldn't afford cassettes, so we bought blank tapes and sat for hours next to the radio. As soon as we heard a song we liked, we hit the "Play" and "Record" button at the same time. My cousins, the surgeon's kids, didn't do that. They had actual stereos . . . *in their rooms!*

I knew we didn't have a lot of money. We hadn't moved from that little apartment, and I didn't have a lot of toys, but we weren't starving. When I walked home from school through the field behind our apartment complex, I would stare at the ground. Every day I was sure that was going to be the day I would find money on the ground. I found change all the time, but I was searching for the big prize. A five- or ten-dollar bill! I even made deals with God. "If you help me find money, I will do this."

My parents were on a mission to improve their lives, saving every cent they made and working all the time. Maybe that's why we never talked. When my fourth grade teacher kicked me with his wooden leg or spanked my butt with his paddle, I never told them. What would be the point? I didn't tell anyone. Nothing had been easy since leaving Iran, so this was just par for the course.

The teacher was finally fired. Kids were literally getting hurt in his class, so they had to let him go. Finally some good luck!

And then, more good news: we were moving into a nicer apartment in our complex, away from the tiny, sunken apartment we had all been stuffed into: the "penthouse" as it was described to me. We were moving into the *penthouse* of the complex. (Later, when I was an adult, I visited this complex and realized it was basically a subsidized housing complex).

Our new apartment had two floors. I was so excited I could barely stand it. We started moving into the penthouse . . . but we didn't get very far. All of a sudden we were moving again.

CHAPTER 7

Welcome to Gurnee

I don't know if I even said good-bye to any of my friends in Joliet. I don't remember the teacher wishing me well or telling the class that this was my last day. I don't remember anything. I only remember that it was in the middle of the school year again.

My next vivid memory was standing at a bus stop on my first day of school in my new town, Gurnee, a small town about an hour northwest of downtown Chicago, where I lived one of my disappointing days as a child. (Remember my description in chapter 2 of the football game and surprise move?) It's famous for an amusement park called Great America (which was later renamed Six Flags). My new bus stop was directly in front of our new house.

My parents were renting an actual house, with a garage and everything. (We didn't stay in that first house we rented very long, however. But I didn't have to switch schools when we moved again. We would live in three different houses over the next three years. We kept moving for some reason. I didn't ask. Honestly, I didn't care).

It was also at that bus stop that I got into my first fight in Gurnee. There was another boy at the same stop every morning. He hardly said a word. Maybe he was shy, and he wasn't bigger than I was. So I picked on him, saying rude things and seeing what kind of reaction I got. The more I picked on him the more power I felt.

Then it happened. Eventually me needling him went from words to an actual fight. I remember shoving him in the chest with both my arms. Then, like a blur, I was down. Without much effort on his part, he had kicked my ass. I still think of that kid. I'm actually so glad he kicked my ass. He didn't deserve me acting out on him the toll the last two years had taken on me.

That was not my last fight. It also wasn't the first or the last time I picked a fight unprovoked. It didn't take much to set me off, and I got into several fights over the next year. Eventually the principal of the new school called my parents in to meet with him. I was causing trouble on the bus and in the school. This was the first sign of the beginning of my anger issues.

I became less of a troublemaker, however, once I found baseball, football, and basketball. My love of music continued. I was in love with the Police, Foreigner, and Loverboy. I was playing drums all the time. Tony (whom you met in chapter 2) and I were inseparable. The only thing he ever did that pissed me off was make fun of my Persian-American accent on the bus one day. I remember the incident well.

We were on our way to school, and I was telling a story to the other kids on the bus. In the story I needed to make a knocking sound to describe something. I made the knocking sound, but I did it the only way I knew how: the Persian version, which is *tagh tagh tagh.* Tony and the other kids thought it was hilarious. I remember the pure shame. The incident was embarrassing and motivating. Never again would I sound like a foreigner.

When we weren't in school or hanging out, Tony and I also chased money. Once we were old enough, we babysat. Eventually we needed more money to go to Great America. I begged my parents to buy me a season pass to the park. It was $39.99—that I remember clearly. I assured my parents if they just bought this one thing, I would not ask for any more money. They bought the pass, but I was responsible for all the extra costs, like food or video games. That's why Tony and I started to mow lawns. We worked just enough to have arcade and food money at Great America.

If I thought I had been happy in Joliet or in California, I *know* I was happy in Gurnee, all because of my friends. They were everything to me. I didn't have any family in America and my parents were never around. My only family was my brother. As I mentioned earlier in the book, he is four years older than me and we are very different. He acted like he hated me. I couldn't understand it. He was so smart in school, but he never wanted to help me with my homework or show me how to do anything. Asking for help was like walking on pins and needles with him. He had a way of always making me feel dumb.

I often wished I had a big brother who would take care of me. A big brother to lean on for support. Someone who could help me navigate through the whirlwind that was our life in Iran and the United States. There's a song I heard later in life by Coldplay. I can't always listen to it because it makes me cry. It's called "Talk."

Oh brother, I can't, I can't get through

I've been trying hard to reach you 'cause I don' know what to do

Oh brother, I can't believe it's true

I'm so scared about the future, and I wanna talk to you

Oh, I wanna talk to you.

I don't think ill of my brother. He was living in the same whirlwind I was. He was dealing with his own issues, and that wasn't easy. I think in some way I was the "boy" at the bus stop to him, quiet and weak. A good target for someone who needed to throw a few punches. He and I just didn't have the tools to understand our dynamic at the time. As an adult, I don't blame him, but back then I felt like I had nobody on my side, including my brother.

We moved to Gurnee because my parents had bought a small burger place, a Yankee Doodle Dandy, with the help of our surgeon friend (my uncle).

The purchase was a double-edged sword for me personally. While I was finally able to satisfy my insatiable desire for burgers, I also had to work at the Yankee Doodle Dandy. My parents barely had any employees. To make the restaurant profitable, they cut costs where they could, including headcount. My parents worked every single day, open to close. My brother and I were pretty much left alone except when we were working at the Yankee Doodle Dandy with them.

I don't think the restaurant was a monumental success, despite my parents' commitment. For example, to make more money, even while we had the restaurant, my dad even became a trucker for a while—driving the kind of semi-trailer truck that goes across the country and is gone for days and days. I went on a couple of tours with him. I loved the food at the truck stops. I spent most of my time in the sleeper compartment with the curtain pulled closed, minding my own business, listening to music.

On the weekends, my brother and I had to work at the Yankee Doodle Dandy. I hated my shifts there, which sucked, apart from the unlimited burgers. My parents mainly brought us in to help with the lunch rush, but we had to stay all day because otherwise they had to drive us those twenty minutes back to our house.

One afternoon I was attempting to mop the back of the restaurant. I wasn't trying very hard and was probably goofing around a little. I hated that task; I hated being at the restaurant; and I hated being away from my friends. So I accidentally knocked over the bucket, spilling water all over the brown, grungy floor.

Next thing I knew I felt a burn in my butt from a swift kick in the arse, courtesy of my dad. When we lived in Iran, I would be spanked occasionally, but my parents had never laid a hand on me in America—and they had definitely never kicked me. The only other time I was ever kicked in America was by my fourth grade teacher with the wooden leg.

I didn't cry. I never cried. My parents hated tears. I cleaned up the water and went behind the restaurant to do what I often did. I got my tennis ball and threw it against the brick wall, imagining I was a pitcher for the White Sox. I imagined I was Richard Dodson throwing curveballs to Carlton Fisk.

I spent most of my time at Yankee Doodle Dandy making up elaborate daydreams and acting some of them out. I was either getting dumped by a girl I loved or recovering from a bad play in a basketball or football game. Whatever the scenario, the fantasy would end with me battling through, overcoming the terrible thing I was facing, and ending up a hero.

I must have had a thousand dreams I lived while mopping the floor or taking out the trash at the Yankee Doodle Dandy.

CHAPTER 8

The Secret

I don't know why, but I had an urge to tell. It was the early '90s. I was driving from Champaign to Chicago with my dad. I was in my mid-twenties.

I have no idea why I brought it up. Maybe it was because my mom was in Iran visiting her family. My dad and I didn't talk very much. Not because we were at odds; it was just the way our family was, even as I became an adult. We talked about the weather, business, and the basics. Never about how we felt or what we thought of the world. Never about important stuff, like who I was.

I am not sure even today that my parents really know who I am. It's not intentional or malicious. They were simply limited in this arena. I realized these limitations, studying the dynamic between my dad and his dad when my grandfather visited us. I carefully observed their interactions, or lack thereof. I am certain they went days without uttering a single word to each other apart from, "Dinner's ready," and other even more trivial exchanges.

My dad had accomplished a great deal since his life had been uprooted and he had had to start over in America. I can appreciate the challenges he faced and the things he overcame after leaving his country of birth. I'm certain my grandpa never acknowledged his son's achievements. I'm sure he never told him he was proud of him.

My dad and I were talking about the importance of family. My mom was in Iran to see her brother and sisters. My mom was the only one in our family who could safely travel to Iran, and so she took advantage of her mobility every chance she had.

My dad put a huge emphasis on family. I didn't get it. To me, if you don't talk and connect, then who cares if you are from the same blood? I didn't agree with loving someone just because you are supposed to. I hated when my parents would call a family member in Iran and then hand me the phone to talk to them. What do you talk about with someone who doesn't really know you but is your uncle or aunt? I hadn't been around any family for years!

I would listen to my dad talk to our relatives on the phone and there was very little actual conversation taking place, nothing that was relevant to what was going on in our lives. The conversations were simple, inane. They would go back and forth asking how the other person was and then go through the names of everyone on that side of the family and ask how each one was doing. This would go on for the entirety of the conversation. A weird checklist of family status that revolved around the physical health of everyone and the weather.

And yet, my dad believed family was everything. Perhaps he was right. But at the time I couldn't have cared less. I had no real family in America except my dad's very young brother. He was closer to my age than my dad's. He lived with us for a few years in Gurnee. Like my dad, he also became a trucker. My best memories were going trucking with him or working at Yankee Doodle together. When we moved to Champaign, he followed us but finally got his own place.

I loved him more than anyone in the world. He was not only my uncle, he was also my best friend. He probably doesn't know this or realize how important he was to me. He seemed to love me unconditionally. Then he left to start his own life in California. His leaving me hurt as badly as any of the moves.

I was disappointed when my uncle left but never upset with him. He left because he needed to get on with his life. He got married and moved away. I'm sure he has no idea what he meant to me. I was a master of making sure no one knew my true feelings.

The conversation in that car ride with my dad began to turn into a lecture about family and why I should care more about it. My dad didn't understand my aloofness toward family. Not only did I not care about family for the sake of family, I also hated to be told how I should feel about anything.

So I decided to tell him my secret. I just wanted him to know why I couldn't care about people just because they are family. He listened closely as I told him the story. I told him the abbreviated version. There was lots of silence. My dad literally did not say a word, and when I was done, I quickly changed the conversation for his sake. And that was that.

My parents don't do well with these types of conversations. Jeckel and I talk about this all the time. My mom couldn't stand when my brother or I was sick. She was limited in her ability to see us *imperfectly* without her projecting her own fears and expectations.

When I was sick or upset, my parents internalized it into their own pain. Their childhood injuries were played out in my suffering. It was also a bit cultural. The success of Iranian kids plays a huge role in the self-esteem of their parents. It is a very proud culture, and mistakes or blemishes reflect on the parents more than in any culture I have ever known.

After that day, my secret was never discussed. I am certain my dad must have later told my mom, but to this day no one is even the slightest bit curious about what happened. No one has ever asked me about it or tried to understand how the abuse affected me.

It started when I was about eight or nine—not long before we escaped from Iran. He was my older cousin—the cool older cousin. My mother's sister's eldest son. He had a motorcycle. He was a tough guy. Mansoor was his name. I remember him as a rebel. I remember one time he and my dad got into it. It was close to a fistfight. I vividly remember this. My dad threw him out of the house. We weren't even at our house. It was at another family member's house. Don't know why they fought. Didn't care . . . didn't ask.

Mansoor lived with his mom just a couple of minutes from us. I hung around him all the time. He sometimes even bought me stuff. I wanted this toy helicopter; you pulled a string and the thing would fly. It was so cool. I wanted one. He said he'd get me one. And that's when it started.

Don't remember the details of the first time. (Or I

conveniently choose to forget the details?) I do remember the place. It was in the mechanical room of the pool in our compound in Isfahan. It was dark, musty, and dirty. I basically just lay there as confused as an eight-year-old can be in a situation like this. He was my older cousin, he was supposed to love and protect me. This was the opposite of loving and protecting me. I think he was eighteen or nineteen at the time, but to me he was a giant. An actual grown man. Not a kid! I didn't really have a choice.

As you would expect, I still have so much of this blocked out in my head. I remember having to take my pants off. I remember him lying on top of me. I remember feeling like I was being crushed. I remember exactly what he was doing. It didn't feel good at all. I also didn't have a choice. The whole thing lasted ten minutes at the most. Once he was finished, he would simply go back to being my cousin. And that was that.

I remember every time. But what I don't remember is what I thought as I exited that mechanical room. I would give anything to know what I was thinking. It's possible I wasn't thinking. So, I just went on with my day . . . soccer here I come!

I never told anyone. I never even thought about telling my parents. And that wasn't because of the warning I got from him to not tell my parents. It was because I never shared anything with them in the first place. It wasn't useful or productive. I thought it was my fault. And frankly I assumed I would be blamed for this somehow. I could have said NO. I could have screamed. But I did nothing. I just accepted it. Shame on me!

The next few times were no big deal. I was used to it and completely deadened. It was as routine as kicking a soccer ball with my friends. I remember basically just being dead. It was like, *Okay, let's get it over with.* But I did try to avoid him as much as I could. I hated his face, but I was a little boy and never showed it. I hated when my mom would have him come pick my brother and me up from school. Not only would I have to see his disgusting face on those days, but I would also have to go to the mechanical room.

Luckily, my dad was almost assassinated, and we had to flee Iran. For me it was escaping hell! The war, the train ride, and moving were easy compared to that bullshit!

I didn't think about this for decades—I mean, decades. I never told a soul. I think I told Andy, and I told Jeckel, of course. It was completely blocked from my mind. Didn't dream about it, didn't have weird thoughts about it. Literally it was like it was erased from my memory until I found it again in therapy.

I have one lingering trigger that remains . . . I still get a weird feeling when I hear the sound of a belt buckle unclasping. The metallic dangling sound gives me goose bumps. Every time I put on a belt, I think of this. It was that sound I remember in the mechanical room, the sound of the belt coming off, and I will never forget it. It is etched in my memory.

I love going through my parents' old photo albums. I've learned so much about myself and our life back in Iran through those albums. One of them had Mansoor's picture in it. But it was him as an adult. I think he was maybe even married with children. Those poor kids!

The first time I saw his picture was tough. I formed this fantasy. It was basically the adult version of me going back to Iran and finding him. I would take him hostage at gunpoint. I would ask him who else he had done this to. For every one kid he mentioned, I would put one bullet in his leg.

Then I would wait and look at him. Look to see if was in pain. Look to see what his face looked like when he was in pain. Would he cry or beg for his life? I just wanted to see the look on his face with me in complete control. I also wanted him to see how angry I was.

I didn't want him dead—that would be too easy. I wanted to torture him. I wanted him to beg for his life. I wanted to see him beg for me to stop putting bullets in his legs. I wanted him in pain. A lot of pain.

In some ways, I have always wanted to tell my mom. I really wanted her to know what a creep her nephew was. I assumed my dad would be the messenger to transfer this news. But . . . crickets! Nothing from Dad and certainly never a word from Mom. How could my mom not want to talk to me about this? Is it possible that my dad never told her? And if he didn't, then why not?

This pattern was just symptomatic of the world I lived in. It hurt me deeply knowing that this terrible thing which had happened to me would never, ever be brought up again. Shouldn't they want to tell me how bad they felt for me? Or, at the very least, acknowledge the wrong, and comfort me? To this day, I have no idea.

CHAPTER 9

Mr. Popular

Leaving Gurnee was the worst experience of my life. I can say that honestly, even with all the trauma and upheaval I had seen in my life to that point. You'd think I would be used to upheaval by then, but nothing I had been through prepared me for the pain I felt leaving Gurnee.

I had never hurt so much. It was worse than leaving Iran in the midst of a violent revolution. It was worse than my experience in the mechanical room with my cousin. In Gurnee I had found stability. I had friends who made up for my dysfunctional family. I had an identity: I was an athlete and I was popular. With no warning my life had been turned upside down.

In Champaign I was lost and alone. But I never cried. I know sometimes that's a promise kids make to themselves when they are trying to seem tough or cool. To me, it was real. I was incapable of crying. I am not sure if I could have broken that promise even if I had tried. The part of me that was able to cry was "out of order."

My parents and I moved into in a small two-bedroom

apartment in a complex called Hessel Manor. Back to an apartment; back to a life with no escape. My world figuratively and literally got smaller again as the walls of our tiny apartment closed in around me.

My parents immediately started working. My mom got a job first at McDonald's and then later at Bob Evans. My dad did odds and ends jobs while working toward opening his own business. My parents had sold their Yankee Doodle Dandy and were upgrading their business to a bigger and better one. They just needed to save a little capital.

The new business was the only thing that made me feel hopeful. I didn't allow myself to get too invested, but maybe, just maybe, this would be the business that would change everything. Maybe this would be the business that would get us into a house again. Maybe this would be the business that would make me feel secure.

I was tired of being poor. I hated being told "no" to things because we didn't have the money. I am sure my parents felt the same way. We hadn't been financially comfortable since fleeing Iran. Being immigrants and leaving our old lives behind meant starting from the ground up.

I think this is part of what drove my parents: not just the pursuit of wealth, but overcoming their shame at what they were—immigrants. In Iran we had had status. My father's Western education and job as the head of the factory meant that we were affluent. Everyone expected that my dad would go far. Then came the revolution, and all those dreams and hopes were shattered.

I think what inspires many immigrants to be successful isn't the rosy-colored wish to live out the American Dream. Sure, everyone is grateful for opportunity. But I think what it really gets down to is shame.

Shame might drive immigrants to incredible success, but the side effects are ugly. My family can speak to that firsthand. The need to achieve and overcome the shame left scars on their kids and themselves.

Things were rough outside the home as well. Moving in the middle of freshman year was a bitch. By the time the school year was halfway done, all the students had already settled into their social circles. I had a really tough time making friends.

I'm sure some of my issues with making friends were due to my own emotional state. I wasn't in the best place. I figured everyone was already in a group, and I was tired of starting all over again. When I saw kids hanging out and having fun, it made me think of *my* friends back in Gurnee, the only home I had known in a long time. I really missed Tony. I missed him terribly.

My new classmates had already made their memories together. I would stare at a group of kids standing in a circle outside the school. They looked so happy, laughing and poking fun at each other. I could feel their laughter in my heart. I wanted to be able to laugh like that again. I *wanted* someone to come poke fun at me. I was so desperate I'd even have welcomed someone making fun of my accent, like Tony did on that bus.

Every day felt worse than the one before. I kept to myself for most of freshman year.

Across from our small apartment was Hessel Park. The park had a hoop court. This became where I spent all my free time.

Once again I had to resort to sports as my refuge. The guys who hung out there weren't the same kids who went to my high school. These were mostly young black kids from the neighborhood, a similar demographic to the neighborhood I had lived in, in Joliet.

I knew how to get along with people from any background or skin color because I wasn't white and I knew it. It didn't hurt that I could shoot a mean three-pointer. We were out there every day playing basketball, and I even had a nickname: "White Larry Bird" (make sense out of that one). The hoop court in Hessel Park was what got me through my freshman year.

My parents were busy building their life.

They only cared about my studies and my grades, whether or not I was a straight-A student. They equated education with success; my mental state was never part of their formula for success in life. If I got perfect grades and went to a good college, I would be rich and respected. All I knew was that the good grades I was getting weren't making me happy.

I imagine most teenagers have a difficult time connecting with their parents. Maybe it isn't unusual that my parents' interest in my life was limited to what grade I made in History. I was a sensitive kid, though, and I internalized the lack of questions as a lack of interest. I thought my parents didn't care about me.

I am not even sure I realized this consciously. Every child needs attention and emotional mirroring from their parents. Every child needs to feel unconditionally loved. My parents loved me, but even as a kid I knew there were conditions attached to their love. I worried about it every day, wondering where I stood. Every day I spent time analyzing what grade I was getting from them.

They didn't do it intentionally. I think it was their way of motivating me. My dad didn't say he loved me until I was in my thirties. I am sure his dad never uttered those words either. He was just following the same parenting he received from his father. I don't blame him.

Finally, it happened. I wasn't totally surprised. It had become my mission. I was done feeling sorry for myself and feeling like shit all the time.

I was in my sophomore year Chemistry class. I had been partnered with a girl named Shannon, one of the popular girls. She was friends with all the cool kids.

I did something silly with those little tubes. I accidentally broke them, creating a small fire. The next thing I know she's laughing so hard she's crying. I had been noticed. She laughed at my joke, and I was literally giddy. Making people laugh had been my specialty in Gurnee. It was like I had forgotten this skill, but that day I remembered why and how I was good at making friends.

I took full advantage of that moment. My confidence and self-esteem were on the rise, and I started making friends left and right. One day when I was at the basketball courts, I noticed a guy who went to my school playing tennis. He asked if I had ever played. I hadn't, so he invited me to his house and showed me a video of John McEnroe playing at the U.S. Open.

The man was swinging his racket like a lunatic, smashing the plants around the court. It was amazing. I used to think tennis was for preppy rich kids, but this video changed everything. Tennis looked like something I could get into. I started playing—and fell in love. I was addicted. I practiced day and night. By the time I was a senior, I was one of the best players in the state. Being one of the better tennis players in the state didn't hurt my popularity either. But it gets better!

I met Andy . . .

Our friendship began just after a Friday night basketball game at my high school. Our team was playing our crosstown rival, where Andy was a sophomore. The gym was packed; every seat was filled. I was there to watch the game, but at halftime, the cheerleaders picked me out of the stands to participate in the halftime show. I knew ahead of time. I had agreed in a heartbeat—I loved the attention.

I went out to center court. They offered me a basketball. I grabbed the ball and launched it from half-court. *Swish.* Nothing but net! The crowd went *nuts.* I had just made a shot from half-court in a packed gym in front of our rivals. And I was drunk! (Back then it didn't take much. Like most high school kids, I had just started experimenting with alcohol at the Friday night house parties my friends would throw.) Holy cow. I won a year's worth of pizza from Domino's.

The next day, the doorbell rang at my apartment. It was Andy. Tall and handsome—definitely a ladies' man—I knew who he was, but I had never met him.

He said, "Wanna hang out? I have a car."

Those were his exact words. The rest is history.

Andy and I have been best friends since that day. We were inseparable in high school. Then we went to the same college.

He was my best man. We still live in the same town. I see him all the time. He was one of the only people who knew about the extent of my issues.

My friends, especially Andy, cared about what I did, what I thought, and how I felt. My popularity became increasingly important to me. When I lived in Gurnee, I hadn't realized I was popular. I just sort of lived and didn't analyze why I put such an emphasis on having friends. In Champaign, I spent a lot of time analyzing my relationships, my friendships in particular. I had made it my mission to not be lonely. I made it my mission to be known. Being popular was my lifeline at the time. Being well liked was the foundation of my self-esteem. Having attention and being liked wasn't a *want* but a true *need*.

It only took a year, but I actually started to like going to school every day. The second I got home, all that changed. I lived split lives. I had my world in compartments, perfectly organized.

The way I got through my time at home was TV. The second I got home I would run to my parents' bedroom. They had a black-and-white TV on their nightstand. I would watch show after show until I went to bed. Anything from *Different Strokes* to *Family Ties*. When I think about it now, there was definitely a theme in the shows I watched: they were all about families. More specifically, families that communicated and seemed normal.

I would fantasize about being part of those families, that the TV parents were my parents. Those parents asked their kids questions and talked about how their days went. I wanted to be Theo from *The Cosby Show*. He and his parents seemed really interested in each other. These were never conversations that happened in my home.

My senior year was the best year of my life to date. Everything in my life was going well: The girls started liking me for more than just being their buddy. I was doing well in sports. I was the guy you wanted at your party. I was fun; I'd happily sacrifice my body for a laugh. Just laugh at me and I'll jump from a bridge. Laugh at me and I'll finish this case of beer. I didn't care.

I moved back and forth through so many groups then. I circulated among them simultaneously. I played with jocks. I played with the progressives. I played with the nerds. I played with the burnouts. I played with anyone regardless of skin color.

I partied a lot. We all did. It was the happiest time of my life, and I could do no wrong. My parents left me alone, and I got more and more wrapped up in the buzz I got from my social activities. I couldn't get enough attention. I never got tired of partying. And I was developing an insatiable appetite for both.

That year, when Homecoming came around, I was voted King of the Homecoming Court. That's how far I had come: from the sophomore with no friends, desperate to make kids laugh in Chemistry, to the Homecoming King of the school. I had made up my mind to be popular. As a senior, I had done it. I had achieved what I set out to do. I wanted to belong. I wanted affirmation. I wanted people to love me. To me, at that time, being Homecoming King captured all those things, including love.

That got my parents' attention. All they had really cared about before was grades, but I could tell they were proud. They told all their friends. I am not sure they actually knew what being Homecoming King meant, but I was in the newspaper and wore a crown. I was a *king*. I think they missed their Shah, their king back home in Iran. And now I was temporarily their king.

Senior year went quickly. As the school year sped to a close, I began to feel sadness and anxiety. The idea that high school would be over was not easy.

I was voted "Most Popular" by my classmates. When I walked through the hallways of Champaign Central, I was home. There was a role reversal between home and school: School was home. My high school family was so important to me—I had worked so hard for it—and I was about to lose it all.

The best time in my life was ending. I would have to start all over again, as I had done so many times before.

CHAPTER 10

A Red Corvette

A red Corvette convertible. That's what I was riding in. I was the King. I was sitting there in the open air, people on both sides of the street. They were clapping and smiling. Staring at me like I was important. For hours, street after street . . . Why?

I wore a silly crown on my head (the one I got my senior year of high school) parading through the streets of Champaign, home of the Fighting Illini of the University of Illinois! It was Homecoming weekend, and I was invited to ride in the parade along with the U of I Homecoming King and Queen.

I remember thinking, "I'll do that, too, in four years. I'll be the Illinis' Homecoming King. Why not?"

It was a cloudy October day. October was the month I moved to Champaign. It was also around the same time I came to California from Iran. I have struggled with this month for a long time. Jeckel and I talk about how I get anxious and even more depressed in October.

It sounds strange to say, but to me, October has a distinctive smell. That smell always triggers certain memories and feelings.

It did then, too. Summer is usually beautiful and green, and then fall comes—I remember noticing the leaves on the ground, discolored and out of place on that terrible drive from Gurnee to Champaign—and everything starts to decline. Moving from high school to college, I felt the same sense of decline. I was eighteen and I felt the best was behind me.

Graduation was a buzzkill. I remember the last couple of days of high school. Signing my friends' yearbooks and having mine signed. It was terribly depressing.

"Parham, you're awesome . . . what a senior year . . . we'll be friends forever . . . blah blah blah . . ."

It was over; we were all separating. The strange thing was that my friends were excited to go to college. *What is wrong with everyone?* I thought. Maybe they didn't need high school as badly as I did. I wanted to be in this place forever. I was never more comfortable in my life than when I was in the hallways at Central, laughing and joking with my friends. My teachers even liked me and laughed with me. I was the King!

The worst part was that Andy was going across the country to Arizona. Almost no one from my high school that I was close to went to U of I.

As depressing as graduation was, we still had one last summer together, and it was epic. My cousins, Andy, and another one of our close friends rented an apartment on campus. These "cousins" were the kids of some of my parents' friends in Champaign, another Persian family. When we moved into that apartment it was the first time I had lived away from my parents. It was only for two months, but we had an amazing summer.

My best memories were of my cousins and me throwing parties that people actually paid to come to. We formed a production company and started a band called Noillim Looc. That's "cool million" spelled backward. We would rent park district facilities and throw huge parties. Our band was always the headliner since it was the only band that ever played. Sometimes we had a DJ.

We sucked as a band, but we knew how to throw a party. More importantly, we knew how to convince people that this was a party they needed to be at. We gave people their money's worth as we supplied them with enough booze to last a whole night.

For example, one night we rented out the Urbana Park District Civic Center for $500. All week we sold tickets—about 350 tickets at $20 a pop. Do the math. We'd fill a tub with Everclear and punch and put it out. We used this mixture so the Park District employees wouldn't know we were serving alcohol, since Everclear has no odor or color.

We even did a show in Chicago. Somehow we'd talked our way into being the production company for a huge Persian event at the Aragon Ballroom, a famous venue in the Windy City where famous performers like Sting came and played. I remember sitting backstage and toasting to the fact that we were sitting where U2 had been just a few weeks before.

I'm not sure how we got this gig. We heard this event was going on and I guess we knew someone. They hired us to do production: lights, sounds, and effects—things we had never done before. We just faked it. We went to a local place in Champaign and rented equipment off a list of requirements the band managers had provided us with. We loaded up a U-Haul and drove up to Chicago.

The event was huge. A few thousand people had come to see performers like Shahram Shabpareh, the father of Iranian pop music. The opening act was Andy and Kouros, a famous duo from California. We handed them their wireless mics and they went on stage. Only problem was we had forgotten to put batteries in the mics. They came off stage and started yelling at my brother. My cousin and I ran out into the back alley and split up to go hunt for batteries. Bottom line: We never got another gig.

That same summer I decided I wanted to play tennis for the U of I. Even though I had been playing tennis for only three years, I was burned out after State. Most college players had played for a decade or more by the time they graduated from high school. The coaches thought I needed to see this through because I had a lot of potential. So I decided to walk on.

Our first workout was in the middle of August just before school started. It was hot and humid. We were doing suicide drills in the middle of Memorial Stadium where Illinois played their football games. We finally finished what seemed to be hours of running.

After that we proceeded to the weight room. We partnered up and were handed a sheet with the workout schedule for the afternoon. I did the first set. Excused myself to the men's room. Puked my guts out—spaghetti from lunch. Then I walked up the stairs without even grabbing my stuff. I left the building and headed for the parking lot. Got in my car and headed to Andy's. Got to Andy's, exchanged a couple of words, grabbed the bong (not something we did regularly yet), and that was that.

Money was tight, so after that first, epic summer between high school and college, I had to move back home and live with my parents. (I paid tuition with financial aid and loans.)

I noticed that all the other kids were having a ball in their freshman dorms. I noticed that people were quickly making friends and totally engrossed in dorm life. Not me. I lived at home and it was a totally different picture.

I felt like I went to college, but I wasn't a college student. I was very isolated from the college experience. My self-esteem couldn't have been lower. My popularity in high school had allowed me to suppress all the issues from the past, kicking the can down the road. I was about the crash from the high.

Going to class in college was also totally different. I used to walk into my high school classes and be greeted with high fives and hugs. Now I was just one of forty thousand students. I had some classes that more than a thousand kids attended at one time. No one knew me or cared to know me. I never talked to anyone. I didn't try. It wasn't worth it.

I had a goal in high school to be popular. In college, I didn't have that goal. And I didn't want to go through that whole thing of making friends, making people like me again. I was exhausted. I didn't feel like being "on" and building a new network.

I had my cousins, and that was good enough.

I had used all the energy I had to get me through high school. I had lost it. And so went my confidence and my self-esteem!

The dancer slows her frantic pace

In pain and desperation

Her aching limbs and downcast face

Aglow with perspiration

Stiff as wire, her lungs on fire

With just the briefest pause

The flooding through her memory

The echoes of old applause

I loved that song—Neil Pert was a genius. He wrote the lyrics of most of Rush's songs. I studied lyrics. There are so much wisdom and so many lessons in good lyrics.

I was curious as hell why he'd written those lines about an aging dancer who was slowly becoming irrelevant and watching her talent fade. I have no idea why I paid such close attention to the hidden meaning in lyrics. But I did. In this case, I was the dancer. I should have felt like I was in my prime with my whole life ahead of me, but it was the opposite. I was on my way down. I was only eighteen.

I still study lyrics. I know the lyrics to so many songs and I use them to help me identify with my emotions and think big philosophical questions. They also serve as emotional bookmarks to my life. Many people don't know this about me.

I was obsessed with this song. I couldn't become the dancer. I was too young. I had to try harder.

I joined a fraternity. I really don't remember how that came about. I didn't live in the house, but I went to all the social events. The fraternity thing was fine. I met some cool people that I still consider friends. The folks I was attracted to were older and big partiers. Room 16! That was the party room, occupied by a few juniors and seniors that liked me. And I liked them!

Our fraternity house was split between the Room 16ers and the Preppies. I gravitated to the first group, the stoners. I was introduced to drugs and thereby found a new fix for all the complicated emotions I felt, especially the sadness. Very quickly, my appetite to deaden myself grew at an exponential pace. Next thing I knew I was doing all kinds of drugs: acid, mushrooms, whip-its, and weed.

As a result, freshman year was a blur. I was in a drug-induced fog most of the time. I never went to class. I would deaden myself with drugs and booze and listen to music. I became fond of acid. I was using every day.

I learned a lot about people and myself on drugs. I analyzed those around me and of course myself. People would show their true colors when taking substances. I felt they were reduced to their core "character" on drugs and booze. I watched closely. I was often disappointed by what I saw. I became more and more isolated the more I analyzed people.

So many of the guys and girls I met were fake. I hated fake people. I hated selfish people.

The first two years of college I was in aviation school. You don't get a degree in aviation, but you do become a commercial pilot. I wanted to be a commercial pilot from the day I can remember. I wasn't on a lot of planes as kid, except going back and forth to Iran. I would watch the pilots. So cool and respected. In the early eighties they were like heroes. And of course they had a harem of ladies following them, the stewardesses.

But, my pursuit of a commercial pilot certification didn't go well. I was immature and forgot why I was there. I basically flunked most of my non-flying classes. I just wanted to fly and had no desire to do the classwork.

Then one day my freshman year I lost radio control and forgot how to communicate with the tower because I hadn't paid close enough attention in class. I was stuck in the air circling the airport for an hour. I was terrified.

Eventually I quit.

Enter reality.

I got a letter after my first semester, the gist of which went something like this:

Dear Parham,

Your first semester of your first year of college is a complete disaster. You are dumb, uninspired, and a flat-out disappointment to this university. Get your shit together!

Sincerely,

Dean of Liberal Arts and Sciences

I was put on probation. I had a GPA of 1.6 out of 5. I failed two of my five classes. I looked at it differently: I was passing three out of the five classes!

The next semester was no different than the first. Lots of partying—chicks, guys, and *me*!—but similar disappointments in others and myself. I still really missed my friends from high school.

Looking back, I hung around many people. I even laughed a lot. No one suspected I was unhappy. Around other people I acted happy and was very social. I was usually a lot of fun.

When the party ended, however, I was in my own world, alone at home listening to Rush, Depeche Mode. Rush because of the deep nature of the lyrics, and Depeche Mode because it connected with my sadness. I listened to this over and over:

Let's have a black celebration

Black celebration

Tonight

To celebrate the fact

That we've seen the back

Of another black

Day

On nights like those I'd go outside and look into the sky. I'd talk to space.

I don't know who I was talking to when looking into the vast sky. I would just talk. Ask questions. Was it God I was talking to? I would hear back, "It's gonna be okay . . . you're gonna be okay . . . you're gonna be great."

Looking at the moon and the stars inspired me then and inspires me now. Somehow looking into the sky reminded me that my problems are tiny and there's gotta be more to life than this!

That gave me some peace. It also helped advance time.

Then reality struck again. I got another letter:

Dear Parham,

We warned you. You are a complete buffoon. You are hereby expelled.

Sincerely,

Dean of Liberal Arts and Sciences

I got kicked out! An actual letter that said I was gone. I was terrified. It was real, and there was no way I was telling my parents.

So I didn't. I met with a counselor. She told me I had only one way to get back into school. I had to take four full-time classes at the local community college, and I had to get an A in every single class. I had no choice. I got my shit together during the summer after my freshman year and lived and breathed school. I got an A in every class. I got back into the U of I.

CHAPTER 11

Another Letter

I was now a sophomore. Almost getting kicked out was terrifying . . . and a wake-up call. It didn't turn things around for me, but it kept the desire to "not get kicked out" at the forefront of my thoughts. There was no way I was going through that again. Four classes in one summer with the pressure of having to get an A in all four was one of the hardest things I'd accomplished.

Andy transferred out of Arizona and came back home to the U of I. I had a few close friends in the fraternity by this time so I talked Andy into joining the fraternity as well.

Fraternity life wasn't exactly my thing. Guys farting and naming their farts—I hated that. Guys stumbling over each other and throwing each other under the bus to impress the chicks—I hated that too. I was so disappointed to see guys turning on each other to impress a girl. I was loyal and proud. I couldn't play that game. I didn't fit in at college like I did in high school and I noticed my relationship with anger being revived.

I had a temper, always did. I didn't think about why. I got into fights a lot. I had learned to fight and defend myself in Joliet, when I was nine, ten years old. That was a rough neighborhood.

I can recall that within a few weeks of my family moving to Joliet, a kid from the apartment complex attempted to bully me. Most of the residents in the complex were black, so I stuck out. This kid made fun of me for being from the Middle East. He actually called me a Pakistani. I hated that.

After about the third time he called me that, I walked up to him, looked him in the eye, and nicely reminded him that I wasn't from Pakistan; I was from Iran. So he laughed, called me a "Pakistani" again, and seconds later he was on the ground begging me to stop hitting him. Living in Joliet taught me not to be afraid of confrontation. Nothing scared me and I would never back down to anyone. Never.

Looking back, I see now that there was a trigger. Fairness! Most of my fights, the raging temper, were triggered by the feeling of getting fucked, the feeling that something was unfair.

Back to college, my sophomore year.

It was a typical weekend. Andy, some friends, and I were at one of the campus bars. It was packed. We were sitting at a high-top table in the bar area. It was early in the night.

Andy was a gentle giant. He's a big guy, every bit of six feet three inches, but he doesn't have a single mean bone in his body. He wouldn't hurt a fly, and he didn't like conflict.

We were sitting there, minding our own business, when this big steroid-head walked by Andy and bumped him. We thought nothing of it and continued talking. Minutes later, the guy did it again. And then again, and again.

"You know this punk?" I asked Andy.

"Nope, and I don't care," he said.

This is bullshit, I thought. *If he's not going to say something to this jerk, then I will.* It wasn't fair.

So I asked nicely, "What's your problem, asshole?"

I don't know what he said, but he gave me a little shove. I got up to shove him, but before I could even get a chance to push him back, he threw his beer bottle at the center of my chest.

I remember thinking, *What the hell is wrong with this guy?* I had a flashback to the kid that kicked my ass at the bus stop in Gurnee. Maybe this guy was as crazy as the guy who beat me up as a kid. I was never worried about someone being bigger than me. The only character trait that I feared was someone that was potentially crazier than me or had nothing to lose. I stayed away from guys like that.

We were immediately grabbed by a bunch of bouncers and out we went.

Now outside, I noticed the punk walking across the street, heading the other way. *Bullshit,* I thought. *We aren't getting kicked out for no freaking reason just to see this coward walk away.*

So of course I started yelling for him to come back and finish what he'd started. Andy wasn't happy with me. I should have walked away. It was a dumb idea.

Here we go. Now we are in the alley. Brick walls surrounding us on both sides: the bar on my right and a Laundromat on my left. It wasn't long before he was on top of me, pounding away. He was a lot bigger than me and had me on the ground in no time. He really wasn't even landing any punches, but neither was I. As I lay there I heard Andy yelling at us to stop, and I heard a voice inside my head: *Just get up, just get up . . .*

Somehow I got up around his grip. A few people started gathering around. Who doesn't like to watch a fight?

I got my bearings. The rest is awful. I was able to hit his head against the brick wall and it was over. I couldn't stop hitting him. Then I heard police sirens and it was time to go.

Next thing I remember I am sitting in Andy's car. He's yelling at me. I couldn't believe he was mad at me. Like I said, he's a very gentle man. Andy didn't like this side of me. He didn't understand where my anger came from. He couldn't relate to it, and he didn't approve of it.

Andy was and is a great friend. He was calm and relatively grounded, even at that age. I knew I needed help with my temper. It was problematic. So, he and some of my buddies talked me into boxing. They handed me a flyer for a boxing tournament and said I needed to do this. I put my need to punch people to a constructive use.

I took up boxing. The tournament was a few months away. I decided to get in shape: I quit drinking. I quit taking drugs. I went on a crazy diet. Even when I was playing sports in high school, I had never liked training. I never worked out except for playing the sport itself. I hated conditioning and lifting.

I had never lifted weights seriously. I needed to get stronger, so I decided to join a gym. I walked into the nearest one to join, and I couldn't believe what I saw. I almost turned around and got the hell out of there. Too late.

The guy greeting me was a trainer at the gym . . . and he was *the guy from the fight* in the alley. He had stiches on his head. He knew exactly who I was.

After a very awkward few minutes, I told him why I was

there. I told him about my anger problems and why I wanted to lift weights. He smiled—and that was it.

A unique bond developed between us. As we became friends, I told him my life story. He soon knew about Iran, about all the moves. We spent a lot of time lifting weights and talking. Eventually the only thing he didn't know about was my cousin Mansoor, but no one did.

I was perfect for months. I worked out nonstop. I was manic. I lifted, swam, ran, and boxed every day. I was in the best shape of my life. I was ready to beat the shit out of someone in boxing ring, an "Andy approved" venue.

The fight was at the military armory. I didn't know we even had one in Champaign. The place was packed—standing room only.

They announced my name. Earlier in the week I'd had to pick a song that they would play when I entered the ring. Just like the pros. It wasn't easy to pick the song, but after much discussion with Andy, we chose "Relax" by Frankie Goes to Hollywood.

My song came on. I was standing next to Andy and my trainer in the hallway looking at the ring. People to my left and to my right. We were basically in the chute, just like you see on TV when a pro fight starts. My heart was racing, and, truth be told, I was nervous as hell. *What if I get my ass kicked like I did at the bus stop in Gurnee?* I said to myself. At that time there were only four kids who saw me embarrass and shame myself. Tonight, there were thousands of spectators.

Then, all of sudden, it was pitch-black except for a spotlight shining on Andy and me in the hallway. Everyone was staring at me as I made the fifteen-second walk to the ring.

Then I was in the corner and my team was trying to acclimate to our corner and the environment. Andy and I were clueless, but not my trainer. He happened to be the defending champ from the previous year. He was a friend of one of my cousins and volunteered to teach me how to box. I knew how to fight. I didn't need help with that. But boxing, that was an entirely different thing.

Ding, ding, ding. I was off!

First round didn't go well. I hardly landed a punch, and I couldn't breathe. I had trained nonstop for months, but nothing could have prepared me for the kind of shape I needed to be in.

I remember talking to Andy and my trainer between the first and second rounds. They told me I had hardly thrown a punch. They also told me that my opponent had thrown about thirty punches. I remember thinking that Andy and my trainer don't have a clue and how wrong they were.

They were right, but the good news was that the other guy didn't land many punches. For every three proper punches landed, you get a point. He was only up four points. He had hit me twelve times.

Ding, ding, ding. The second round!

I start dancing around the ring. My nerves were a bit more under control. I was ready to prove to the hundred or so friends who had shown up that I deserved to be here.

Trying to look like a real boxer, dancing around, I got too close to the edge. My foot slipped.

The ref immediately ran up to me and put himself between my opponent and me to stop the fight. I wasn't being penalized for slipping; the rule is that a boxer gets free clearance to get up.

When the ref stops the fight, the opponent has to stop and move away. Not this asshole. He ran up to me while I was trying to get up and hit me—right in the middle of my head, from behind. That wasn't fair.

I snapped. I jumped up, locked eyes with him, and chased him around the ring. It was a full-on street fight now!

Mayhem. The ref jammed himself between us. He wanted us to *stop*.

I was in a blind fury. I went crashing toward the asshole who'd taken an unfair shot at me when I was on my knees. It was all frenzied chaos and—smash!—I got the wrong guy.

I hadn't meant to! I was trying to hit that punk. Instead, my fist had connected with the ref who had been trying to split us apart.

I was disqualified, and that was the end of my boxing career.

CHAPTER 12

Twenty-one Days

I didn't dwell on the loss. I should have and could have beaten that asshole . . . if he'd fought fair. He went on to win the tournament. That part did hurt. I could have beaten him.

Spring break was just a few days after the fight. I went to South Padre Island with a bunch of my frat brothers. Some of them I barely knew.

I don't know why I went. I just couldn't get into the spring break thing. Sure, it was wild, and I was kind of a wild guy, but I just didn't fit in. Going on spring break with a bunch of insecure guys battling for chicks was exactly what I didn't want to be doing with my time.

But I did. I had lost my fight, one of the only things I'd really put effort into since starting college. So on that spring break trip, I reversed course. I did exactly the opposite of everything I had been doing for the last few months. I partied with nothing to lose.

Something else had changed too. I loved partying before, but part of what I loved was the social element. I like either being the center of attention or sitting back and analyzing people, figuring them out. Now I partied with a sense of sadness and loneliness. I partied to forget and to kill my thoughts.

As I mentioned in the last chapter, in training for the fight I had been *perfect*. I treated my body like a temple. I did not have a single drink. I worked out four times a day. I drank multiple protein shakes. I even ate freaking cottage cheese, which to this day I can't stomach. I was incredibly disciplined. I never went off script.

I even went to class. I had straight A's going into spring break. And we had just a couple months of school left in the semester afterward.

All that was about to change. I don't remember how it started. But I do remember everything else about those first few weeks after we got back from South Padre Island.

Quick backstory.

My sophomore year I felt I needed to live away from home, having spent my entire first year of college at home with my parents. I decided to live with one of my pledge brothers, John. He and I lived in this really old apartment above a sporting goods store on campus. I started teaching tennis on the side, just enough to pay the rent.

John was a star swimmer from the East Coast. Good-looking guy: tall, with a typical swimmer's physique. This guy was a real ladies' man. I was anything but. In high school, I had lots of girlfriends and friends who were girls. In college, I literally had zero. From day one I couldn't even talk to girls. I was just not very confident. It was like I missed that train.

John and I were alike in other ways, though. He was a lot

like me when it came to his appetite for partying. He was also a lot like me in that he was lost, maybe even more lost than I was. We were well-known in the fraternity, and some of our frat brothers made fun of us. They thought we were derelicts.

While I knew at the time that I wasn't a complete derelict, I did also realize that this was my new way of getting attention. Once I gave up on being the popular kid from high school, I took on a different role, a new persona: a druggie who wanted more booze, more drugs, and more fun. This Parham got his attention by creating events that made people laugh not because I was funny, but because I played the fool.

John and I were clowns. People liked me, but for the wrong reasons. Ironically, I was the mature one in our duo. Even though we were the same age, I was the big brother, the voice of reason.

It was a weird relationship. He came from a wealthy Connecticut family. His parents were very sweet and they were very fond of me. His father was a successful businessman, and they thought I was a good influence on John. For some reason I must have given off that impression.

John was a bad drunk back then, and so I had to look after him. Most evenings I was guiding him home. By midnight, you could barely understand a word out of his mouth, but I loved him just the same. It's fair to say we had a codependent relationship.

I wasn't the most fun roommate before my boxing debut, but that all changed after my return from South Padre Island. I made up for my lack of partying at school the second I returned from spring break.

I woke up every day to the sound of the gargling from John's little three-foot bong. It was red and had Grateful Dead stickers plastered all over it. It served as both my alarm and a metronome of sorts. The gargle from the bong was a steady rhythm that managed our day.

We'd meet in our little living room every morning. Our ritual was a bong hit, our way of saying, "Good morning." We'd sit on the wooden floor on top of a rug. We had no furniture. Not even a couch. We had pillows and a little TV set on the floor. Then we'd smoke weed until Bogart's opened.

Bogart's was a store literally thirty feet from our front door. It was a head shop that sold all kinds of paraphernalia. Bongs, one-hitters, and everything burnouts required that was legal. The only time I would leave the tiny apartment was my daily visit to Bogart's for supplies. From the day I got back from spring break I carried out this routine for twenty-one straight days.

Bogart's sold whip-its, otherwise known as nitrous oxide. We'd buy a case everyday and split it. Twelve each. We'd take the cartridge, put it in the gadget, and turn. Crack it and the balloon would fill. Then we sucked on it. Not once not twice, but fifteen to twenty times. The more we sucked the more our brains would be deprived of oxygen and the more we'd hallucinate.

John and I did this for hours. We'd take a hit of the bong then immediately follow it with the balloon. I was told that thousands of brain cells are killed on every puff. I don't know if that's true, but I do know that by lunchtime I was toast.

We'd sit there for hours and not say a word; just stare. Our brains were burnt. The ride was wild. I remember to this day the

feeling of being completely brain-dead. I became mute, cata-
tonic, and deadened.

There were no groceries in the apartment. I ordered Grogs
pizza every single day. Each pizza cost $3.83. I was somehow
conscious enough to write the amount of the check in the ledger of my checkbook. I remember showing the ledger to some
of my friends and bragging about the number of consecutive
debits for $3.83 . . . the phone call to Grogs happened two or
three times a day for twenty-one straight days.

I don't know what was going on with me. The only thing
I can think is that it was a routine, the development of a new
ritual. It was a distraction. It felt right. I felt dead.

That's what I was craving or needing. No different than a
workaholic—or any "holic" for that matter. When our minds
are consumed with a single thought, we shut off everything else.
The question, is what are you shutting off? In my case, I had no
idea.

Looking back, it was truly amazing how I went from one
extreme to another. In many ways, it was who I was—it was
me. Whenever I did something, I did it with total commitment,
whether it was tennis, boxing, being popular, or getting back
into school. Whatever I chose to focus on had my full attention.
Which is why, when I was in a destructive phase, I was fully
committed to the destruction of myself with a grand spirit and
a relentless fervor.

CHAPTER 13

Twenty-one Days Later

When I woke from twenty-one days of hell and the fog slowly lifted, I entered a new phase diametrically opposed to the previous twenty-one days.

I was running out of money and I was about to fail all my classes. That was the realization that I woke to one day. I had straight A's before spring break but I hadn't been to class for three weeks. I had missed several tests and assignments and was completely lost in school. I had flunked out before, and I knew that if it happened again, I had zero chance of being reinstated.

Anything I did for a long time, good or bad, made me nervous. In some ways, I was conditioned to adapt to constant changes as opposed to consistency. This was a perfect example of a short period of multiple transformations: from student to boxer to druggie all in three months. Obsessively taking care of my body as a boxer and destroying it with pizzas and drugs had the same underlying psychological premise. Now, with the consequences of my bad grades looming, I had no choice but to abandon this current cycle.

I reengaged as quickly as I could. My only goal was to salvage the semester and not flunk out. I went crazy—and it paid off. I completed the semester and salvaged a bunch of C's. Better than F's but worse than the A's I had going before falling off the face of the planet.

The semester ended and I moved back home. That summer I taught tennis every day—hours upon hours. I was loving it. I was making money and doing something I was good at it. Little by little my popularity as a coach grew. The popularity was a boost to my self-esteem, so I pushed it. I was teaching all the time. I spent all my waking hours studying the game. I read book after book. I analyzed everything I did. I was thirsty for knowledge about the game and sought it every chance I had. So, I lived and breathed teaching. My new obsession— my new addiction.

While I loved teaching anyone regardless of their age, I especially liked teaching kids. Kids, anywhere from six to high school age. We understood each other. I was able to easily connect with the kids, and I loved seeing them happy. I felt I'd had a positive impact.

As time went on, my reputation kept building. I was in demand. My kids were getting good. I had never experienced this type of pleasure before. The attention I was getting was for a skill I had, the impact I could make, and not for being funny or popular. I was actually respected by the parents of these kids. The kids liked me for the help I could give them.

I spent the next few years focused on teaching. I was still going to school, and I wasn't partying like crazy, other than the occasional normal kind of partying that a college age kid did.

I went out on the weekends but never depended on it. I took teaching very seriously. And I took the relationships I had with the kids and their parents even more seriously. I was connected. I felt a purpose. I was *happy.*

There was a subconscious shift in my thinking that happened during this phase, too. I don't know if it was maturity or the responsibility of the job (or both), but I reengaged with my big-picture thinking. I was managing my day-to-day with more intention and started looking for a purpose to my existence. The first couple of years in college were a blur of nonsensical thoughts. Now I was back to looking into the stars and sky for direction. I began to dream about bigger and better things.

Tennis was giving me some direction. The connections I had with those kids were genuine and real. I thought obsessively about ways to make their tennis game better. More importantly, I wanted to make their lives better. I wanted to give them confidence. I wanted them to feel important. I wanted them to feel happiness. I loved them, and they loved me back. In many ways, this was unconditional love: a new thing for me.

The connections I had with these kids changed my life forever. I remember hearing the way the parents of these kids spoke about me. They referred to me as an enigma—I remember because I had to look the word up. They were intrigued as to why as a twenty-year-old I devoted myself to these kids instead of going out and having fun like a normal college kid.

"Why does he care so much?" I remember overhearing. I placed those kids' needs above mine. I even gave up my weekends and traveled with kids to tournaments. To me it felt altruistic, and I had never felt that. I wanted nothing from them.

I liked making money and I liked watching them win, but it wasn't about that. I just had this need to make a difference in their lives. Maybe I was acting out a wish I had for myself that went unmet. It was like a religious experience or awakening.

Thinking about my purpose in this world led me to thinking a lot about religion. We fled from Iran because of our religion. I had strong feelings about organized religion: I didn't get it. But I always felt that I had a certain relationship with a higher power. I thought about this all the time. I couldn't understand why all this universe would exist without a purpose. There had to be a greater cause or reason for everything.

I was content during this time. All the anger and pain I had felt—they weren't eating me up in the same way. I was at peace. This was a phase that would last seven years.

I listened to a lot of Midge Ure, the lead singer of Ultravox. He was a great humanitarian. You can see that in all the music he produced. Song after song illustrated his loyalty to humanity and a bigger cause. I deeply shared his values at this time. I really cared about others more than myself. I worried and thought about the poor, the hungry, and the oppressed. I wanted to do good and make a difference too. I listened to this song over and over. It was humbling:

Give me, love for the lonely
Give me, food for the hungry
Give me, peace in a restless world
Give me, hope for the children.

Because I was living at home again, my parents witnessed the endless hours I devoted to the kids I was teaching. While I was paid very generously, I still did a lot of stuff for free. I remember my dad once questioning my lack of desire for money. My answer was simple: "I'm happy! That's all I care about, Dad."

I also remember saying that I didn't care what I might do in life, I just wanted to be happy and love what I was doing. And if being a garbage man or tennis instructor was the thing that made me happy, then I was going to keep doing it. I was very idealistic at that time in my life.

My dad's perspective wasn't misguided. My parents, while doing a bit better, still worked their asses off for some future day that they dreamed of. They had opened and closed a restaurant, and my dad had justed started in the automotive repair business. Their immigrant mentality was still strong and their fear of scarcity was high.

Our relationship hadn't gotten much better. Even though I lived at home, I didn't see much of them. And when I did, it was superficial. We talked about the basics like food and health. I wanted to share so much with them. I wanted them to understand how important I had become in so many kids' lives. I wanted them to see how much respect I got from the parents of these kids. These were doctors and business professionals who put a lot trust in me, the kind of people my parents would respect.

My parents, whether they would admit it or not, had a lot of fears regarding my decision-making and my future. Back then they didn't think I was too smart. My brother was the smart one. He was a genius, going to grad school to study astrophysics: this after getting a degree in physics and computer science. He was a human encyclopedia. He specialized in everything. I'm not exaggerating in the least. He had a brilliant brain inside his skull.

Me, not so much. I wasn't booksmart and didn't read anything I didn't have to. My parents feared I wouldn't amount to anything. My confidence in the presence of my parents and my brother was low as a result.

What was happening away from home was having the opposite effect, however. I was becoming more and more in demand. I had a huge following as a tennis pro. It eventually got to the point where I could pick and choose whom I taught. I was also able to pick my price. Although I didn't do it for the money, I was well compensated. I don't think there was a pro in town who was paid more than me—and I was still a college student on the five-year plan!

One of my counselors inspired me to think about my future. She encouraged me to think about the potential of going to graduate school. The disaster that was my first couple of years as an undergraduate could be wiped out with a strong last two years.

She told me that my last 60 hours of credits would determine if a graduate program would take me. So, I pretty much got A's those last 60 hours. She assured me that a graduate program was going to focus on how you finished your undergraduate courses as opposed to the first two years.

I continued to follow a good pattern of behavior and grew serious those last two years of college. I continued to work and travel with a group of tennis kids. The group of tennis girls that

I worked closely with for many years would eventually land at the same high school with all them overlapping for a couple of those years. I decided to not only teach them year-round but also join forces with a good friend of mine who was their coach at Centennial High in Champaign.

Illinois tennis was dominated by the wealthy Chicago high schools. But, something was about to happen that changed our tennis community forever. Those girls went on to win back-to-back state championships! It was unprecedented. And I had played a role in that.

It was an accomplishment for so many involved, and I was a big part of it. I had never really accomplished anything like this in my life. The combination of successes—but, more importantly, the impact I was having on the lives of these kids—made me seriously contemplate teaching tennis as my life's calling. At this point, I was certain this was what I would be doing for the rest of my life.

But, I met a banker.

CHAPTER 14

I'll Show You, Part I

I remember sitting in Andy's room on his bed, talking while
he got dressed and made himself pretty for a night out on the
town. It was 1994, my final year of college. It was also my fifth
year there.

Andy lived in an amazing house that his parents had bought
for him to use while he was in college. It was two stories—
with a basement—in a nice neighborhood just off campus. I
was envious of his setup, as were many of our friends. And like
them, I spent a lot of time there. I might as well have lived
there. But I lived at home instead, to save money.

The second floor, his room, was a loft. He had a giant
bathroom and tons of closet space. He had a killer stereo, so
sometimes we'd just party up there. Our conversations were
usually light: We talked about girls, made fun of people, and
told stories.

But I remember this one conversation very vividly. Not the
details of the conversation, but everything else. It was like a tug-
of-war but without the rope.

The words out of my mouth were about the future, serious for a twenty-two-year-old. His responses would tug the conversation the opposite direction. I'd ask, "What are your dreams, Andy?" and he'd say something like, "Dream on *this*." You get the gist. He wouldn't allow the conversation to go any further.

At one point he was telling me, "Stop it!" I remember this because I made a note of it in my head. I remember thinking he was uncomfortable. I felt like maybe it was me; something was wrong with me. *Am I kinda turning into a nerd? Getting too serious . . .*

I also remember thinking that I hoped Andy and I weren't losing our compatibility. Maybe we weren't in sync anymore.

Our timing was definitely off. I know the future made him a little nervous, and he simply preferred to not talk about it. I was as nervous about the future as he was, but I processed my fears differently than he did.

Two things happened that year that really affected the direction of my life. The first came from coaching tennis and the other from a local banker.

As I described in the preceding chapter, I decided to help coach my old high school tennis team. I did it mainly because there were some girls on that team that I coached year-round. I couldn't be the head coach since I didn't teach at the school, but I could be the assistant.

The boosters got together and raised money to pay me a generous salary. The money meant nothing to me. I was more interested in the impact I was able to have on both their game and their lives. The success I had teaching was important, not just with the kids but with what was happening outside the lines: the relationships with the kids' parents.

It meant a lot to me to have the respect of these grown-ups. They were doctors, professors, and lawyers. Imagine yourself as a little child, staring up a your dad or mom. They'd look like a giant to you. That's how I felt around these parents. They were like giants to me. From my vantage point they were important, successful, and smart. And they respected me and actually listened to me. That mattered. It was something I wasn't used to.

I was as grateful to have these adults in my life as I believe they were to have me in theirs. They were like family to me. They believed in me and supported everything I did. What mattered the most was that they made me feel important.

I needed that badly. My parents at the time weren't terribly optimistic about my future. I never heard those words directly from them, but I was very good at reading between the lines. They were always telling me about so-and-so's kid who was going to medical school or law school.

They would use indirect signals like, "Did you know Ahmad is going to medical school and he's going to marry Mariam? She is going to be a lawyer. She's so beautiful and comes from such a good family." It wasn't hard to figure out what they were really saying.

Their subliminal lack of support for the passions I was currently pursuing wasn't malicious. They had their own desperate needs that were being projected on me. My parents' vision for my future was crystal-clear. So clear, in fact, it was mapped out on a piece of paper: a graph my dad had drawn for me about nine years earlier.

I was in ninth grade, still living in Gurnee. It was football season. My parents hated football and hated me playing football. They have never seen me play football, nor had they asked me what I did or how well I played. If you asked them now, they still wouldn't know. I took it well and blamed it on the fact that they worked so much.

If that didn't work, I rationalized that maybe they didn't like anything that didn't resemble soccer. Football and sports in general were not something that the culture valued or recognized. In Iran, no one became highly respected because of their ability to use their hands or feet in sports. Either way, deep down, I got the message loud and clear.

I was in the living room when my dad asked to talk to me. He had a piece of paper with some stuff written on it. On closer inspection, I saw that it was a diagram with a long horizontal line extending from left to right the length of the paper. And on every inch of this horizontal line were smaller, perpendicular lines extending downward. Next to each of the smaller lines was a number . . .

The first number was fifteen—my age at the time. The numbers got greater as you went from left to right. It finally dawned on me. It was a timeline of my life. Right there in front of me . . .

In detail, my dad explained the chart of my life. Not my life to date, but the chart of my life in the future, starting from this year. He went on to describe a section of the chart that was small, a chunk that depicted a time frame from now until I was twenty-five. A short ten years.

He then showed me a much longer time frame. That was the line from twenty-five to seventy-five. He said that sacrificing the next ten years would then provide me with *fifty years of happiness in the future*. He said that if I gave up playing sports and playing with my friends now, I would be happy for the rest of my life. As if sports, friends, happiness, and financial success were mutually exclusive. He added that only a very small number of people make it in professional sports, so my chances of success were very low.

This timeline conversation was the result of a conversation we had had a few days prior. I had told him I wanted to be a professional athlete. This graph was his way of discussing my future options based on my dreams.

I never forgot that chart. It affected me in so many ways. Back then I didn't have the tools to analyze my feelings about it. I just had one thought: I'll show you!

Back to the early nineties. I was approached by the father of one of my tennis students. He was one of parents I had tremendous respect for. I went to the meeting assuming he wanted to discuss his son's training.

I was greeted and escorted into a beautiful office by his secretary.

"Hi, Parham. We've been expecting you. Can I get you anything?"

I told her I was fine.

I sat there patiently until he approached. I stood up, shook his hand, and sat down. Now nervous, I listened. As he started talking, it was clear that he had called me in for a very different reason than to discuss his son's performance.

He started telling me about all these wonderful characteristics I had. He told me I was a winner and so likable and how those characteristics are a winning combination in the real world.

Yikes, I thought. *What the hell is going on?*

Then he went on to say something I'll never forget. "You know, you'll be great at whatever you decide to do. You're one of those people."

I was dizzy, flooded with emotion. I felt hair after hair slowly rise on my arms.

Then he went on to tell me about his business. I don't think I heard a word about the business or what he did. I was still in shock. All I could hear echoing in my ear was "You are a winner."

I did hear the word "job," apparently. He wanted to know what my future plans were. What I wanted to do when I grew up. I told him that I wanted to have my own tennis institute. He told me, if I wanted, he'd find a place for me in his company. No matter where he placed me, he knew I would move up. I awkwardly thanked him and said that I was grateful for the meeting.

I left that meeting happy. No, I was elated. I left that meeting floating out the door and soaring back home like a bird. Soaring like "White Larry Bird."

That meeting touched me on many levels, the most obvious being that maybe I had some value that people noticed outside of my tennis skills. It was also a conversation I had never had with anyone up to that point. I also remember relinquishing any fear about the future. It dawned on me that no matter what I did or where I started, I would be successful. Sadly, I've never seen this man since.

Around that same time, graduation was approaching and I was thinking seriously about my career. I loved tennis, and I was good at it. So, I thought about continuing to explore tennis as a business. I loved it and already had a huge following in place.

The plan I eventually concocted was to open my own tennis facility and start a local academy, a training center. I started the process with the help of one of the tennis parents. We built a business plan and figured out how much money we would need.

Business plan in hand, I went to one of the local big banks and met with a banker. He wore a white starched shirt with his initials engraved on his cuffs. He had cufflinks as well. He was wearing khaki pants and a black belt. He listened to my plan. He even nodded positively many times throughout my spiel. Once I was done, he smiled. He said that they would do the loan, but that I basically needed either someone rich to guarantee the loan or a serious amount of collateral.

My business plan didn't matter, whether it was viable or not. My character, past accomplishments, and having the tennis community behind me didn't matter. All that mattered was that an adult, one of those giants with money, would cosign the loan. All that time and effort wasted . . . I wish I had known that before I spent all that time describing my vision to this asshole.

The shame and hurt I felt cut deep. It was painful. I hated it. It resurfaced every insecurity I had. Was it because of my name, a Middle Eastern guy in the office of the whitest man on earth? Or had he seen through my façade and figured out that I wasn't very smart? What was it? I can easily access just how I felt that day, reliving the shame I felt.

That one meeting triggered a reaction that changed the course of my life.

Up until then, I was an idealist. I wanted to make the world a better place. I wanted to do what felt right and fulfilling, regardless of the financial incentives. I wanted to do something that mattered and something that was meaningful.

After that meeting, I never wanted to put myself in a position to feel that small again. I wanted power. It no longer felt appealing to be a good person and pursue my ideals. All I wanted to do was rid myself of the shame I felt in that asshole's office.

The message was clear. Money was power. Money meant that people listened and took you seriously. Money meant that you weren't laughed at by a man in a fancy white shirt and cufflinks. That day, I made up my mind. I had one goal: I was going to be rich.

I was going to show him.

CHAPTER 15

I'll Show You, Part II

The tennis facility plan was out the window. The banker had squashed all my joy and ambition for that. I needed to come up with something new.

I had quite a bit of money saved up from teaching tennis, about $70,000. It was time for Plan B.

Up north in Gurnee, the Yankee Doodle Dandy that my parents operated was next to an auto repair facility. A Middle Eastern man owned this auto shop. My father had a mechanical engineering degree and was intrigued by the man's business.

Neither the man nor my father spoke English very well. Assimilation had not been a goal for my parents. In their view, they were visitors to America, waiting for the revolution to blow over so they could get back to Iran. It had been more than a decade, and still I think they subconsciously held onto this hope. I knew our stay in America wasn't temporary. They, however, did not.

This mindset isn't uncommon for immigrants who are displaced against their will. The hope of going back is powerful.

You hear about people coming to America in hope of pursuing the American Dream, but I think, in my parents' deepest unconscious, they believed they were eventually going to go back to pursuing their dreams in Iran, even at the tender age of forty-seven.

Despite this, they continued to look for business opportunities in America. Inspired by their business neighbor, my dad decided to invest in an auto repair franchise. So my parents sold the Yankee Doodle Dandy.

Champaign wasn't the ideal spot for the next auto repair franchise. The area wasn't a huge market—not at the top of the franchise's list in expanding their brand and footprint. The Chicago area, where we were living, was littered with opportunity. The franchise had a dominant footprint in the area, whereas in Champaign it would be a totally new establishment. Champaign was risky.

But Champaign was where my brother had just moved to start school. My parents were following him, much to his dismay.

It took several years for the shop to open. This was a remarkable accomplishment for my parents. I remember asking my brother about this business. Was this finally the business that would make us stable? Was this the one that would get me out of that apartment?

The success I had with my tennis business and the realization that I wasn't as dumb as I thought gave me a lot of confidence. No matter how poorly that meeting with the banker had gone, I felt that, in time, I would be successful in whatever I pursued. I knew I could start anywhere on the totem pole and eventually reach the top. That's what had happened with tennis. And I felt that I would find a way to move up this ladder, too, just like my student's father had told me in his office.

My dad had been operating the business for about three years now. It was mildly successful. My parents being the savers they were, always living for the future, made it work. I spoke with him about maybe getting involved in his auto repair business. I knew nothing about cars or what made them go. I didn't know how to put in oil or even where the oil was actually housed in the car. I knew where the gas tank was and that was about it. But it was time for a change.

So, I jumped in. I was still finishing up my last year of school, but I started going to work with him to learn the business. I remember early on thinking that running this business was the same as teaching tennis and also not that dissimilar to throwing parties and concerts. I was good at promotion, I was good at coaching, and I was great with people. It was all about people and coaching.

It didn't take long for my dad to let me have a lot of control. I have always admired him for letting me run with the business. That took a lot of guts. The engineer in him saw things as black and white, which was diametrically opposed to how I saw the world. He was a master of managing money; I was good at increasing money. He had a lot of discipline and I did not. I threw parties!

I was a constant promoter. My dad had just a few employees, but I felt that we could do better. I talked a talented mechanic into joining us by selling him on the big vision I had for the company. I also was a great salesman. It was easy to get customers to like doing business with us. The business immediately started doing significantly better in sales.

I couldn't stop thinking about the business. Like everything I cared about previously in life, I became obsessive. I was at the shop many nights past midnight: painting, remodeling the showroom, or designing promotional materials. The business was all I cared about. What motivated me? That banker came into my thoughts on a daily basis.

I was in my last semester of school. I remember sitting in the Illini union where I often studied with my textbooks piled up around me. Now, however, the books just sat there as I looked at the expenses and sales numbers. I had no desire to study anything that was theoretical. The last semester of school was a joke to me. I was now preparing to be a businessman. I'd sit there for hours thinking about how I could make the business better.

I remember my first staff meeting. At Andy's house that morning, I had typed out my agenda and written a memo for each employee. I distributed the memo to our entire staff, which was three people, plus my dad and I. As ridiculous as it was to write a memo for three people, I wanted to operate like a real business.

My dad didn't say a word in the meeting, but afterward he told me he was proud. These were words I'd never heard in my life from my dad. I always wondered how difficult that was for him, knowing his dad never uttered those words to him.

I know how it made me feel. It was amazing. I also remember thinking I wish he could have felt the same thing I did that night at some point in his life.

My dad being proud of me had a profound impact, but it

got even better. My brother was over at my parents' house one day, and he happened to see one of my memos.

This is etched in my memory. I remember exactly where I was standing: I was in my parents' bedroom, standing by the bathroom. He told my dad to listen to me.

I couldn't believe my brother. He'd just told my dad that he should pay attention to my ideas and opinions. An endorsement that I had never heard all my life: an endorsement that I was grateful for. This touched me on so many levels.

I was hooked.

After graduation, I took $12,000 of my savings from tennis and bought a small house. I also put money I had I saved into the business. I remember sitting on the floor of the new house. I hadn't furnished the place except for a bed and a futon couch. I sat there both proud and scared. I had a $260 mortgage, which at the time seemed scary.

I hope I can do this, I thought.

I dove in and became even more obsessed with the business. Underneath that obsession was my failed meeting with the banker and my dad's chart from when I was fifteen. I was going to prove to everyone that I was smart.

I worked nonstop. I read book after book about business. I met with other owners and picked their brains every chance I got. Meeting with those owners and seeing their shops put things in perspective. There was a glaring contrast between what they had achieved and what we had achieved. Crap, we were in the bottom 3–4 percent in sales.

This opened my eyes. I didn't have much to compare our store to, but once I realized the reality of our ranking among the other stores, the competitive nature in me rose. I refused to be associated with the bottom. I refused to feel ashamed! So this only fired me up more—and helped fuel my drive.

Over the next few years I would become even more serious and focused. I was aging faster than my age. I purposefully dressed old and acted old. I remember a girl that Andy was dating telling me that I was dressing like an old man. I didn't care. I didn't party, hardly went out, and was singular in my thoughts and goals.

I heard this in the back of my mind: ten years of sacrifice for fifty years of happiness.

Crap, I was following the chart.

We opened our second store in 1995. April 4, as a matter of fact. I was on the tail end of juggling two careers. I was still coaching tennis and teaching the original group of girls that I had committed to. I had promised myself and the girls that I would see this through. After they won back-to-back Illinois state titles, I called it quits and just pursued my business career.

I had decided to rent the house I bought. When the second store opened, I was living in a little apartment across from the high school. I was now landlord, and I lived very modestly.

Andy also dove into his business. Like me, he went into the family business started by his grandfather. Most of our friends were either gone or busy with their careers. It was sort of the calm before the storm for me.

I didn't party like crazy anymore, but I did like to smoke marijuana. For me it was an intellectual exercise. I used marijuana to think creatively. I was very productive as result. I repeatedly told Andy about my book idea. Not the one you're reading—the book that lived in my head for a long time that was titled *I Did It All High*, a book about becoming a millionaire by the time I was thirty—and doing it all high! I was serious about it, but I didn't pursue it. I actually worried what my dad would think.

Early in 1996, I remember sitting in my brother's apartment in Chicago with him and our parents. My brother was getting his PhD in physics from Northwestern.. He was married and had a baby on the way.

We had just hit a sales milestone in the business: the $1 million mark. When I got involved, we were doing $380,000 in sales. I was pretty pumped. I remember talking about it with my brother and looking at my mom and dad. They weren't as enthused or optimistic as I was.

"Sales don't matter, it's what you make," my mom said. In other words, it's the bottom line that matters. Ouch!

While this was true, we clearly had philosophical differences. I believed that you would be limited unless you grew the sales of your business. I thought bigger and focused on the long run. I didn't care about short-term gains. They only cared about short-term gains. In some ways I thought they still approached the business like they had the Yankee Doodle Dandy: wrongfully focused on today and what is in the bank now without a real plan to grow market share.

But I was also younger than they were. Their priorities and needs were not the same as mine. They needed the money more than I did.

My thought was that I had to get bigger and build a real company that endured through time. This meant building a brand and a reputation, both things that aren't quickly rewarded. I wanted to own the market, not make enough money to just get by year after year. I knew that later in life I couldn't tell the banker to "fuck himself" if I was just getting by.

I spent a lot of money promoting the business. Then I spent a lot of money hiring better staff. My parents didn't like that. Of course this concern about my strategy was never discussed directly but only through code in the passive-aggressive manner that I was raised with—like refusing to get excited about our first huge sales milestone.

This style of communication drove me crazy. It was such a cowardly approach, and I despised it.

My parents' lack of excitement hurt me deeply. All the goodwill, the early signs of pride I felt from them when I stepped into their business quickly evaporated. The moment from that early meeting with my staff where my dad expressed how proud he was gone. He wasn't proud anymore.

I didn't confront them directly either. My reaction to this was passive as well. I started to get defensive and upset. I had gingerly embraced the idea of my parents being proud of me. It had been a long time coming. Thank God I didn't fall in love with that notion. It was gone as quickly as it came. Once again, their approval being temporary and conditional left a mark.

The following day as we were driving back from Chicago, my mom said, "You should maybe go to grad school."

If you didn't know my mom well, you'd assume this was just about more education or inspiration to better myself, but her true meaning was obvious and clear to me. They were losing confidence in my strategy. Me running the company was making them nervous. Twenty-five years of living with my parents and knowing how they operate clued me in. I could decode anything they said.

So, as usual, we never discussed this again. It wasn't really a discussion in the first place. It was another sentence uttered from my mom's mouth, carefully crafted and skillfully sandwiched in between other sentences. She was a master gamesman. She was then and still is. She grew up as the youngest of nine children from a poor village in Iran, so it's not a mystery where she might have developed these skills and tactics.

I hated the indirect criticism coming from her. What did she know? She was clueless, but I knew she was just repeating what my dad thought and would not say. Neither parent, in my opinion, grasped what my vision was. I was a promoter and a big picture guy; yes, that came at a cost in the short run. I just needed some nurturing and time to make it all work, not unlike the girls I had coached to back-to-back tennis state championships. When they were young, I didn't care if they were winning; I only cared that they were progressing and focusing on the process, doing things that were going to make them great in the future.

I decided to go to grad school. Maybe to appease my parents, maybe to say "F you." I really don't know why, but I'm glad I did. I decided to get my MBA. Surely this would convince my parents I was worthy of their respect and confidence.

At this point I had a major stake in the company, and so of course I didn't relinquish my position as the president of the company. I opened our third store in February 1997 and started grad school six months later, in August.

Now I was even more motivated than ever—and now I had

another chip on my shoulder. I was a bit pissed off, mostly from childhood issues that were being triggered. When triggered, I had a hard time being objective. The lens through which I approached the world got muddied. I would get paranoid and insecure, which was exacerbated by the lack of healthy communication with my parents. It was a cycle I didn't like but was used to.

The third store was a home run . . . enough for some of the tension to subside. Money can do that. The sales of this new store exceeded all expectations. The other two stores had also grown into huge successes. I was now making some real money, as were my parents.

Being the ultimate saver and investor, my dad started building a pretty good real estate business for himself. I think he and my mom were happy. At least they seemed like it, even though I was perfectly aware that this could change at a moment's notice.

I remember standing in their kitchen and them telling me that they appreciated me being involved. One day they are terrified of my involvement and the next day my dad is saying that he now feels like he has a future knowing that I am running the company.

In reality, at the end of the day, we were a good team, from a pure business standpoint: he handled the back office, the money, and the paperwork. I managed and developed the staff, the sales strategy, and, ultimately, the vision for the future of the company. Sadly, if we weren't related, I'm sure we would have appreciated one another more.

I managed to be successful wearing my two hats: as a grad student and as the leader of the company. I had an amazing staff and three great managers who made my life easy. They were all in with my plan and I was all in making sure they achieved their goals. The coaching and people skills I developed were monumental in my management style. Somehow and luckily, people followed me. I was blessed.

CHAPTER 16

Parlennium

I was so sick of the conversation. It was all I heard on the news. It was all anyone talked about. The Millennium! Y2K! It was Armageddon. The world was about to change, and so was I.

Maybe I was naive, but I didn't give a shit. I didn't stock up on canned goods or take all my money out of the bank. I didn't hire consultants to give my business a "Y2K" contingency plan.

Instead, I threw a party. A big-ass party. Parlennium!

My last seven years in the twentieth century had been productive. I was very serious about growing my business. I was focused on opening more stores and eventually being a big shot. I wore clothes more becoming of a forty-year-old rather than a twenty-something entrepreneur, thinking that I would be taken more seriously. I often lied about my age. I remember in particular being at an annual work convention with some of my peers and one of the wives asking, "How old are you?" I said that I was twenty-eight. She laughed and said, "Interesting. You've been saying that every year."

I didn't realize I had been doing that. Apparently pretending that I was older was an important part of my strategy. If that meant dressing the part or padding my age, then that was what I did.

I was approaching graduation from my MBA program. It was May 1999. A lot was about to change.

First, I went on a shopping spree in downtown Chicago, because I needed clothes for my trip to Europe. As part of our international business studies, my classmates and I had a big student project in Germany.

I went to all the places I dreamed of shopping at when I was younger.

I felt anxiety shopping at these stores. I never knew when I would be over my small limit. I'd hold my breath every time they swiped my card. I'd tell myself "Act natural, like you've done this before. Look around, smile, and pretend it's no big deal. Act like you have money." To this day, I still fear that the machine will print out that little slip—"Declined"—and I hate that I've never been able to shake it.

In reality I was doing pretty good: not as well as people perceived or as well as I'd make them believe I was doing. My desire to feed into a perception of my success was more important to me than the reality of where I was. I learned enough about the stock market and my business in grad school to talk a fair game.

It wasn't a total delusion. The tech market was booming at that time, and I was all in. I was an investment genius. That initial success with my investments gave birth to my grandiosity: a slow, methodical, evolving, and drawn-out birth that produced a maniacal, fully evolved ego.

So, while I was buying stylish European clothing and shoes that none of the people my age were wearing (which was a good thing), I also bought my second home, a much bigger house in a much nicer neighborhood than my first one: a truly adult move. This house took on a life outside of me. It had its own character, its own style. It would become ground zero of the new version of my life, a very social life.

Quickly my new home was given the moniker "Club P." The years immediately after my MBA would prove to be a wild ride, a sudden departure from my lifestyle of the previous seven years. Looking back, it feels like I spent a decade at Club P, but it was really only a couple of years.

Ultimately, those couple of years were just another phase of *me* in the struggle to find *me*. This version of me put the cart before the horse. I had a new house, an MBA, and freedom. I thought I had made it. It was payback for the years of being too serious for my age in my early twenties. Ironically, in some ways I had been following my dad's graph, and I didn't want to do it anymore. The fun I was having was payback for the sacrifices I made in building my business and developing my career.

I vividly remember standing on my back porch preaching to friends about an epiphany I'd had. I was a philosopher preaching. I was preaching bullshit.

I spoke about this epiphany with conviction: "If I don't forget about the '*now*' and keep wanting more, then I'll never stop." I was talking about opening new stores, the feeling I'd gotten after opening my third store. I owned a few tire and auto shops. And then I described the feeling of opening the fifth store. It was the same feeling. I was trying to explain that I was getting desensitized.

I thought that each achievement would bring me a new kind of victory, but it all felt the same. I'd desperately wanted to open that third store, that fourth store, that fifth store. But each new opening had me reaching for the next. It wasn't ever enough. I kept waiting to get that sense of heightened elation, but it was all the same.

That saddened me. Success had become relative and my new normal. You want the same feeling, so you need more. That was my epiphany. It holds up as a theory. At that time, it wasn't a bad insight! The only problem was, I wasn't really that successful, relatively speaking. I thought I was way more accomplished than I was. Maybe my epiphany would have made more sense twenty years later.

After I bought the house, I was desperate to have it feel like an adult home. A quick trip to Ikea in Chicago and BOOM! the house was furnished. I wanted it to feel and look modern. Who else owned a swanky bachelor pad at that age? For a guy of twenty-eight, it was pretty sweet.

That's why it became Club P and why everyone would come over to hang out. That's exactly what happened. It was *the* party house. The house became a living, breathing thing with its own cast of characters and dramas and emotions. And I was this living, breathing, but *not* feeling organism entering into a new phase.

The house was given the name Club P as a joke, but it wasn't too far from reality. On an average night I knew about half the people who attended the parties at my house. You could show up at three in the morning, uninvited (like a lot of my guests did), and find a party going on—three, four, five nights a week.

Even if half the people were freeloaders I'd never seen before, the other half of the people were my friends. Half of that half were my close friends. I loved entertaining, whether it was a guy I'd never met or someone I'd known since high school. As long as they were fun, providing for their happiness fulfilled a need I had.

I was the center of fun again. It was like high school, but with better alcohol and better drugs, because of the money I had to buy them.

Club P wasn't in the heart of downtown or in a neighborhood full of students and young people. My neighborhood was filled with families. My neighbors were normal people: professors, businessmen, and teachers.

Club P looked like the other houses. It had a lawn, a backyard, and a garage. But the activities happening inside the other houses didn't look anything like the scene at Club P.

My neighbors were middle class. They woke up, fed their kids, took them to school, and then went to work. They were home by six, walked their dogs, ate dinner, and watched the news. They went to bed at about the time the partying would start. Rinse and repeat. How boring.

Not me. I'd had another epiphany: carpe diem! I was choosing to live a very different life, the most exciting life I could create. I fancied myself a progressive and a modern thinker, more sophisticated than the humdrum people around me. I was refusing to live an ordinary life.

The lenses through which you view yourself can distort the

picture on the other side. I thought I was a self-anointed progressive thinker who'd figured out a better, more fulfilling way to live. What a lie, and what a contrast with the last seven years. My lenses were so off. They were about to become even more distorted.

I was in a small hometown bar, the Tumble Inn, when I ran into an old friend. We chatted for a bit. And then it happened.

I had tried a lot of different drugs. The one I always refused, however, was cocaine. Two reasons why: One, I liked mind-altering drugs—marijuana, LSD, and mushrooms. I enjoyed spending time in my mind and watching the thoughts it spit out. Those drugs altered my thinking, just as they were supposed to, and I enjoyed thinking differently. People didn't seem to think I was crazy; they enjoyed how my mind worked, which made me more confident. My out-of-the-box thinking got me noticed.

Two, I thought I'd get hooked. I had no reason to think I would form an addiction, and I honestly wasn't sure I believed that I would be hooked. It was just an excuse I'd used in the past. I was afraid.

That night though, I thought, *Why not?*

It was a star-filled sky. My friend and I went outside this very small bar into an even smaller parking lot. We went to his car. I didn't really know what to expect or how it even worked. He put a line on an envelope, handed me a straw, and the rest is history.

Immediately after taking my first snort I remember looking up at the stars as I walked back into the bar. I remember thinking that it was the brightest sky I had ever seen. I made a joke that someone had just popped in some new batteries into those stars. *Crisp* is the word I remember thinking at the time.

It got better still. It is crazy how clear the details are, but I recall every step of my walk back to the bar. I felt like I wasn't walking but hovering in a smooth, silky rhythm. I felt like a giant walking back to my seat. I am not tall, but I felt tall.

My breathing was clear. My sinuses were clear. I must have tripled the pure oxygen intake through my nose, it felt so clear. The air was rushing through so smoothly.

I felt perfect. I felt complete.

From then on, cocaine became a fun new addition to my party life. It wasn't the only drug I did socially, and it wasn't a big deal initially because I used it only when Club P was in full swing.

I was working and partying: the best of both worlds. I thought I was the only person who had figured out this balance. My day revolved around two things: work and planning. Working all day and planning for the next party. My phone rang off the hook and I loved it. Today, I hate answering the phone, but back then, I ran to it. I *needed* it to ring!

The parties at Club P evolved in scale at a rapid pace. Sometimes there would be as many as a hundred people at my house. People dancing on the lawn, sometimes just in their birthday suits. People were in bedrooms, bathrooms, and showers. They were doing exactly what you picture people doing in the bedrooms, bathrooms, and showers.

I just roamed the floor, playing host. What a sad and pathetic "social" whore I was . . .

Once it all ended—when the last person had stumbled out, when I had shut the door and turned the lock—I did what I always did. I listened to music and reflected.

This ritual always brought about strong emotions for me. But I never knew what those emotions meant or why I craved them. I couldn't untangle the mess of feelings.

I had a new favorite song. Filter's "Take a Picture." The melody grew on me, and then I fell in love with it once I listened closely to the lyrics. I connected with every word.

No matter at what time or in what I state I ended my nights (which were often, really, mornings), I'd always listen to this song once I was alone.

I didn't play it once and go to bed. I grabbed a stiff one and played it over and over and over again.

While I listened, this mantra went through my mind. *I have an MBA! That's right, a* master's in business. *A decent start to my business career. Suck on that! Who says I'm not smart?*

Then sadness would set in.

One line in the song is forever etched in my mind. As the song builds and builds it all comes together and just at the breaking point, the singer screams in anger and defiance:

Hey, hey Dad, what do you think about your son now?

The first year living at Club P went as fast as lightning, capped off by Parlennium. In my group of friends, I had firmly established an identity as the "moneyman." Little did most know that I had mortgages on top of mortgages to fund all this.

I was doing fine, maybe better in my head than in reality. But no matter how well I was doing, I had the pathological need to make it seem "just a bit" better than it was. Just a little more grand. Hence Parlennium.

December 31, 1999. Like Prince said, "Let's party like it's 1999." What a genius. He knew something about Y2K that we all didn't, decades ago.

To be fair, I didn't name the party Parlennium. A friend did. He was also the videographer I'd hired to come film the party. I wasn't going to throw a party without a videographer. I had this crazy idea to broadcast the party live onto a giant screen that overlooked the dance floor.

Club P wasn't grand enough for the party I had planned. I rented a giant space overlooking downtown Champaign. It was going to be a private New Year's party. The list was capped at two hundred and fifty people. Five hundred would have come had it not been for my security guards. All kinds of people tried to sneak in.

And why wouldn't they? I had steak and lobster served for dinner. The cocktail bar was stocked with a thousand shrimp. I had a DJ and the videographer's live video feeds from the dance floor. I rented limos to take people home or, if you were lucky, to an after-party at Club P. It was Noillim Looc Productions all over again.

The party was a huge success: tons of attention and enough fuel to keep the reputation of the "fun maker" advancing and alive.

It satisfied all my needs in the short run.

I didn't get to listen to my song until much later the next day when I was alone. But when I did, I almost cried.

Hey, hey Dad, what do you think about your son now?

CHAPTER 17

Lonely King

Parlennium was a huge hit. The year after was a blur. Looking back, the math doesn't add up. It wasn't possible to pack that many events, parties, and stories into one year. It's the most challenging period of my life to describe.

I was having a blast. I felt happy, popular again, and getting more popular. And now I was even getting glimmers of recognition and respect. These were new. All clearly important to me.

I had spent the better part of the last decade teaching tennis, working, and going to grad school. Now school was behind me, and miraculously, banks were willing to lend me money, although I never took money from that asshole who had crushed my dreams of opening the tennis institute. I was ripe to take this all to another level.

Hours, days, and weeks were merging together. I didn't see it then, but I lived in the eye of a hurricane. I was a machine. I was the Energizer Bunny who had been introduced to a whole new source of fuel: success and the white powder.

It didn't take long before I was using cocaine every other

day. It really didn't get in the way of anything I was trying to achieve. My intentions were good. I went to work and continued doing what I was doing. I'd come home, party for most of the night, even on weekdays, but I was able to shut it down early enough to be focused at work in the morning. The weekends were another story. Friday and Saturday might as well have been one long day. I partied nonstop, both out on the town and at Club P, but mainly at Club P.

My parties grew bigger, grander, and more famous by the week. I met tons of new people, but I was still closest to my core group of friends. After Parlennium the demand to continue to top the previous party was a welcomed pressure. I loved being the fun maker, the entertainer, and I loved the production.

But, in all honesty, it was the attention that I craved, I *needed*. The attention and the grandiosity were just another welcomed addition to enhance the actual drugs I was taking. I continued to raise the bar. What had been fun and wild enough just months before became, old, boring, and stale.

For example, a couple of months after Parlennium, I threw a costume party for Mardi Gras. I even brought in a live band to play inside my house. The party was well attended by both my core friends and the newbies. The newbies weren't my real friends. They just fit into a peg that matched the hole at the time.

I walked around, a big smile on my face, playing host, and noticing people that I didn't know. Every new face I saw brought up strange feelings; it made me lonely and sad. I felt like a whore. I would give up my soul just to impress people I didn't even know. How sad!

I didn't know this then, but I was very disconnected. I wasn't in touch with myself. I wasn't even really connected with my core friends. I was a machine with needs I couldn't identify, even though I had periods where I was clearly aware that something was wrong with me.

I couldn't focus enough to see what I had: amazing and dear friends. Truly good people—the ones who would stand behind me no matter what. I didn't need to impress them, but I tried anyway. Unaware and ignorant, I couldn't quite grasp the unconditional love they had for me. I was needy even around them. They loved me unconditionally, and they loved me for *me*. They became the family that I always wanted. But that in itself wasn't enough.

The devil powder was becoming more and more a part of my routine. Using cocaine at first was mainly social. It got me to another level—a boost. At first, I loved the boost because it gave me energy and made me feel like a king. That's what kept me coming back to cocaine.

I hid my new habit from my core friends. They weren't into drugs. They loved to have fun, but never went that far. So, in fear of rejection, I kept it to myself. As long as people were around, I felt good about myself. Other people acted as a mirror. When I looked into that mirror, I saw what my friends and these other people saw. The reflection I got from my friends helped my weak self-esteem.

They saw a good person, a generous and genuine person who loved to love. A guy who loved to laugh and a guy who loved to make everyone else laugh too. A guy who couldn't stand sadness. A guy who had radar for negativity. As soon as he'd find it, he'd make it his mission to fix it. He'd always find the positive in everything. I liked that guy, and I liked being him.

When the house emptied, however, I had to look into a different mirror. This mirror wasn't in sync with the other mirror. I saw something entirely different. I couldn't find what others saw in me. I felt ugly. I felt like the immigrant boy who first came to California and was questioned in class about his inappropriate drawings.

No amount of logic could change my opinion of myself when I was alone. It was amazing how unable I was to reconcile the two viewpoints. Two completely different images of myself separated literally by minutes. One view a confident *me*, a well-liked *me*. The other a very insecure and scared *me*.

Even after everyone left and the noise subsided, I wouldn't be alone for too long. I'd grab another drink, I'd put the music on . . . and I'd feel these powerful emotions. I'd sink into some serious, deep, and emotional thoughts. Then, knock, knock, knock . . . here they came, my late-late night friends.

Their timing impeccable, these "uninvited guests" would make their entrance minutes after the stage lights went down, and even though I felt violated, I was completely helpless in refusing them entry.

My demons.

So here we go: another after-after-hours party. My demons started yapping the second they arrived. Their voices were indistinguishable from my voice. Just loud enough for me to hear, echoing in my head.

They cycled through a series of the same old conversations that we'd had hundreds of times before. Sometimes they'd dress all in black. And sometimes they'd dress in clothes from the '80s. They'd want to go back in time and connect with the past, discover what was at the root of all these swirling thoughts and feelings.

I didn't always mind the demons; I just hated when they came dressed in black. My thoughts were dark, then. I had nothing but hate for myself. I hated everything about myself and who I was. When they came dressed in the '80s, I would just lament my time in Gurnee. I'd listen to music that made me feel both sad and happy, melancholic.

On a typical night, especially after a party with a lot of people, I'd sit in my house, disgusted with myself. I'd replay some of the night in my head. I would focus on my actions and behaviors: the things I said and thought. I'd find more things to regret than I would find to smile about. My mind had a knack for finding its way to the dirty feeling of being a whore for attention.

I felt cheap and weak. No one knew this about me. But I did! No one would have guessed that I felt so ashamed and insecure. My self-esteem was bankrupt.

I played this out over and over. I'd be fine while the concert was booming, then I'd crash. I loved the attention, but I hated that I craved it. Holding those two feelings at the same time was so conflicting. I couldn't satisfy both. I wished the conflict gone every night. The only way to make the terrible dissonance subside was to get right back into the whirlwind as quickly as possible.

While a lot of effort was required, maintaining the tornado in me kept the demons out. Keep the train moving forward . . . don't think, and keep the uninvited guests at arm's length as much as possible. Don't reflect. Have another drink and a line.

That song echoed in my head over and over. It got louder and louder and darker and darker.

Hey dad, what do you think about your son now?

I remember being in Palm Springs at a dealer meeting with the other owners in 1997. I was staying at one of the nicest hotels I had ever stayed in. I checked into my room, walked around, lit a cigarette, and stood on the balcony. The view overlooked the golf course and mountains in the background. It was spectacular.

I looked back toward the room and noticed the decoration, the lavish bathroom and furnishings. I felt a wave of emotion. I felt so alone. I thought, *What a shame that I can't share this moment with someone.*

Being in this swanky hotel at this conference gave me a sense of achievement. How'd I get here? This was a long way from the apartment in Joliet. It didn't seem that long ago that I was staring at the ground on my walk home from school, looking for money. What a shame to have this amazing room and no one but me to enjoy it. I couldn't enjoy it by myself. The room meant nothing without an audience.

Without an audience or a companion, I couldn't just enjoy it for myself. Nothing mattered to me that was just for me. Without an audience, it was difficult to find any real enjoyment in anything.

The pleasure I felt walking into that beautiful hotel room only lasted a few minutes. The pleasure turned into sadness.

I met the sadness with one of my rituals. I wasn't in that room but fifteen minutes before I was in the shower. I turned the shower on high and just sat down on the tile floor. Lit one cigarette after another.

I did this for hours. It was a ritual that that was born in Gurnee, but it wouldn't be the only ritual I created to banish sadness. This ritual was the ultimate disconnection from myself and the world.

King one minute, alone the next.

Even when I was king, the undercurrent of sadness was there. It grew stronger every day. It felt like I was living with dual personalities. One of the people was the showman: the man with the plan, the sponsor of so many parties, and the memory creator for my friends as well as myself. I didn't recognize how fake the showman was, that it was an altered state I slipped into. Fake, but natural.

The other person was someone entirely different: the disappointed *me*. He was looking and observing from above with shame. That *me* saw weakness in the little boy that would sacrifice his soul, body, and honor just to get someone to laugh. I was ashamed of the side of *me* that only cared about what people thought of him. That *me* was only as good as his previous laugh or the previous accolade. The observing, hovering *me* saw a little boy that resembled the boy in the mechanical room by the pool in Iran. Dumb, weak, and numb. A whore.

My two selves weren't integrated. That's what Jeckel eventually pointed out.

CHAPTER 18

Here Comes the Bride

I saw her for the first time at my friend Jimmy's place. It was the summer of 1999. Post-graduation from my MBA program and pre-Parlennium. Club P was in full swing. I hung around a lot of people during this period: my core group, the newbies, and the guys I golfed with at the country club.

Jimmy had invited her over to his condo to give her a gift. It was her birthday. I remember thinking she was cute. Young and cute. She seemed really nice and a bit shy, at least with me. She hardly talked to me. I remember thinking, *I'm gonna marry her!*

We had plenty of mutual friends and so we saw each other frequently. We quickly became friends. She was six years younger than me. Very white. A nurse. I remember thinking that she had her shit together for someone so young. She was so independent and confident. *Tough catch,* I thought. At least it would be for me.

We started doing more and more stuff together. She even helped with some of the planning and organizing for Parlennium. We both brought different dates.

We became better and better friends by the day. She was a regular at Club P, but like all my close friends, she never touched drugs or knew that I did. She, like everyone else, always got me at my best.

Thank God for that, because around this same time I started dancing with the devil . . . but, the devil and I, we didn't romance yet. We just slow danced once in a while. Totally social at first but that didn't last long. Soon thereafter I was carefully, lovingly arranging those lines on the bathroom counter.

I remember the first time I used cocaine by myself. I ended up painting my whole house. I mean the whole fucking thing! Every room: three bedrooms, the living room, and all three bathrooms. I didn't stop until it was done.

I used the entire bag and never went to bed. A night of music, booze, and my new friend yeyo. It was a party of one.

In contrast to my core friends, the newbies were the group that liked to party—and by "party" I mean the guys that understood what it was like to stay up all night and paint the whole house the next day. I knew who they were, and they knew me. This stuff wasn't cheap. I had the means to supply it, and so they came.

Everyone at my house was part of the big party. Then the ones coming for the real party, the ones using, had a party within the party. They winked and used code words. We thought we were at the ultimate party, the real, exclusive VIP party. I knew who was part of that party. Their eyes were dilated and their jaws were grinding. They talked endlessly.

Makes me sick to think of it now . . .

The "party" people were always the last to leave. If I hadn't kicked them out, they would never have left.

At some point in the night or morning, I would feel sick to my stomach. I would get anxious and want everyone out. But kicking people out was bad hosting, so I had to use many strategies to get people to leave. Each strategy was unique to the crowd or group I wanted gone. The one that generally worked was when I started cleaning up, putting the booze away and turning down the music. People usually got the hint.

When I was done, I was done, and that meant I the party would end. As my coke habit expanded, I got to the point where I didn't like doing it socially. I wanted to be alone with my ritual and my new friend. In fact, though, I started to hate it. I knew it wasn't healthy, but I thought it was a phase I would outgrow. I'd been through many phases, and I thought this was just like in the others. I thought I had control over when the right time would be to abandon it.

Jen never knew any of these things about me. At the time, I didn't really know what was going on either. I was on autopilot most of the time and didn't analyze too much. But I knew I was lonely.

As I was going through this new phase, I found myself more and more drawn to Jen. She was real, loving, and fun to be around. I didn't need to be drunk or high around her. I was happy around her, no matter what I was doing. I thought that was a good sign. We would go shopping, something I hated normally, and I enjoyed it. We'd just sit and talk. And I'd enjoy that as well. We had become such good friends that I knew if we ever started dating, we would get serious very fast. It began on my birthday, May 2000, in my house, with my core friends. Jen and I kissed for the first time, and thereafter I was committed to taking this relationship to another level. I did everything I could to impress her. I even took Jen to San Francisco for her birthday . . . to show off. Got a fancy hotel and ate at fancy restaurants.

Subconsciously, I was looking for love and a family. With all her amazing qualities, Jen was the perfect person to build a family with. That's when I knew she was the one, and I did everything I could to make it happen.

Things progressed quickly. We had been dating for just a few months, but I decided I wanted to marry her. My family had planned a cruise in December of that year. I took Jen. My parents liked her, once they got over the fact that she wasn't Persian. I had it all planned out. I was going to propose to her on the ship. My brother and parents knew of my plan.

I had been on a few cruises prior to this one; this was Jen's first. All cruises have some kind of welcome party the first night. I contacted the cruise line and made plans to propose during that party with the help of the cruise director.

So here we were in Miami about to board this giant ship. The mood was good. My parents were excited for many reasons. They loved cruises, they loved to see the whole family together, and they loved the fact that I was going to finally get married. To them, getting married meant maybe I was going to grow up. Get serious about life. Persian parents equate marriage and children with growing up.

We got checked in and headed straight to the main deck; a party was under way. Jen immediately started dancing. I remember looking at my dad. He had a smile on his face. He loved to watch people dance. I remember thinking that he seemed to approve of her. I remember thinking that I hoped he was proud of me.

We danced away, the ship still docked. I changed my plans. I wanted to propose right then. It was time.

I talked Jen into going to the tallest part of the ship overlooking the bay. We stood by the railing even though we were high up and it was windy. I was nervous for another reason, though.

I didn't know what words to use. Should I kneel down? Should I hold her hand and go through some corny spiel about how she was my heart or that she completed me? Or something even more dramatic and mushy? That wasn't me.

So, I told Jen I loved her and wanted to marry her. She didn't seem too surprised. I think she had known it was coming. The wind was gusting as we stood at the railing. I reached into my left pocket, and then I raised my arm to show her the engagement ring. I was excited; she was excited.

Then, just like that, the ring was gone. I turned my head to the left and looked down. The ring was falling. Straight into the bay it went.

I need to stop here a minute to tell you that my original plan had been for the cruise director to bring out the ring that evening. We were going to have front row seats at the welcome party. He would tell everyone that he had an announcement to make. Something that would make the crowd roar. He would announce that he had sent a team of divers to fetch the ring that had fallen into the ocean as I was attempting to propose, and then he would present the ring to Jen.

But, it never got that far. I suck at surprises, and I thought the night would be ruined if I didn't act fast. So I reached into my right pocket. Still standing by the rails at the bow of the ship, I took out another ring. The actual ring.

Here came my bride . . .

Hey, hey Dad, what do you think about your son now . . .

CHAPTER 19

Dr. Jeckel and Mr. Hyde, Part I

Roaring down Prospect Avenue at 75 mph. Just a *little* over the speed limit of 35 mph!

Prospect is one of the busiest streets in Champaign, a major throughway connecting the northern and southern parts of town. Prospect was also a direct line from my office to Club P. The northern part of the avenue was all business, but then it quickly gave way to dense, residential neighborhoods. Houses closely lined the street on both sides.

I was sweating profusely and sick to my stomach. My heart was racing, and I was clenching the steering wheel. White-knuckled, I had to concentrate. I had to get my mind off the fact that I needed to throw up.

Wouldn't be the first time. I had thrown up in these situations before: right in my lap or with my head sticking out the window. Such a short ride—crazy. So hard to hold back the vomit. It took everything I had to keep my mind distracted enough to keep it in. It was 8:30 a.m.

I'd been at the office only for an hour or so that morning.

But I couldn't focus. So, as I sometimes did, I placed an urgent call, made up some excuse, and then left for the day.

While driving, my observant self, hovering above, would see a disturbing image. It was scary. My observant self would zoom out, looking down on my car, then zoom out more and see the other cars. Zoom out more and see the whole block. I'd see my car zooming in and out traffic, going twice the speed limit. Screaming past houses, cars, and people on the sidewalk with complete disregard for my safety or the safety of others. Squeezing in and between cars on a drive of less than four miles.

From above I was watching my car bob and weave like the game *Frogger* I played as a kid. I was screaming at the cars to get out of the way. I was screaming at the traffic lights. I took the red lights personally, and they upset me. The screaming would subside the second the light would turn green and then I'd smile.

It was so important for me to get home as fast as possible, not just because I needed to vomit but because something was waiting for me that I badly needed. It was only a ten-minute drive, but the four minutes I could cut from it meant everything.

I timed it so I wouldn't have to wait a single moment. I was a machine operating with perfect precision. My internal clock was tuned to the second.

Finally home, I'd hit the garage door opener and sigh with relief. I'd pull into the garage. Push the close button while the car was still running. Didn't want anyone to see me. Didn't want the garage open a second longer than it needed to be. Get out.

Immediately walk to the only window in the garage and cover it with a large piece of cardboard. I'd even flip the manual lock on the garage. No entry possible: extra precaution to ensure that there was no chance of the garage opening even if someone had a remote.

Walk into the house. Lock that door. Walk to every window, securing them one by one and eliminating any possibility that someone could look in. I did this with rhythm and flow, a cadence that was mastered over time. Every time, every day, the routine was exactly the same. No wasted steps and no action without intention.

Then I'd walk to my bar, take a bottle of whatever—whiskey, gin, or sometimes even just vermouth if that's all I had. I would take several healthy gulps to calm my nerves and start building a base.

The doorbell would ring on cue. From the time I left the office, it was maybe sixteen minutes to the doorbell's *ding*. All the preparation was complete, and I was now ready to greet my hero.

I had several heroes. They were at my disposal no matter what time of day. I made sure to use several people to ensure that a supply would always be available. They knew they needed to be ready as well. They never failed me. When you're spending up to $1,500 a week, they made sure to be there when you needed them. I was a great customer. I demanded exceptional customer service.

I was sick.

What came next was something that happened hundreds of times. I didn't allow myself to reflect too much on it. My observing ego had little power to do anything about it at this point in my life.

It observed something happening that was terrifying, powerful. Yet it was no match for my insatiable need to be with my medicine. It was my lifeline. No amount of logic or guilt could stop this once the trigger was pulled.

Once my hero left, I quickly locked the door behind him. I went to every door in the house for a second time and made sure they all were secured. I went to every window in the house and made sure that every view was perfectly obstructed from the outside. I had this routine down to a science. It had taken time to perfect.

One day, in a sober state of mind, I had walked the entire house from the outside. I peered into every window, studying what someone from the outside could see and where light leaked out. I figured out how each and every blind needed to positioned, depending on the time of day. The process I came up with was bulletproof. I was terrified of a breach.

I did one last lap to make sure I didn't miss any windows, doors, or locks. Sometimes I'd do this two maybe three times. I was so paranoid, so scared that someone would walk in or see me. My ritual was still a secret from everyone.

My locking ritual resembled the characteristics of someone with OCD: no different from someone who repeatedly washes his hands or someone who locks a door exactly three times. That was me when I was preparing. It just all flowed unconsciously without any thought.

Now ready, a smile would come to my face. I felt like a kid on Christmas Day. I felt like Pavlov's dog, salivating with anticipation. The preparation was part of the joy. The routine and ritual were as much a part of the medicating as the medication itself.

I would look at the bag with a romantic gaze and begin to twist open the tie. Would take a whiff. I breathed in pure pleasure. I felt a surge of romance.

I had been thinking about this from the second I woke up, and now it was mine. I lay the contents on my bathroom counter. Fidgety and anxious, I prepared the medicine. A little throw-up would be in my mouth. Sometimes that's all it would be, but sometimes I would have no choice but to throw up before beginning. My body would shake from withdrawal and the anxiety of knowing the fix was close. I would shut off my mind to not feel guilt.

As I prepared physically, my mind prepared unconsciously. It began to numb itself. I was disconnecting, much like I did when I saw my cousin and knew what was about to happen. I no longer had control of me. I was now in the hands of something so much more powerful.

I surrendered my body and mind.

But something would always happen a nanosecond before I'd take that first snort. The pleasure I felt getting ready would shift from excitement to fear: a distinct, powerful displeasure with myself. The pleasure blended with discomfort and guilt. I felt like a whore, so disappointed in myself. So scared. Not sure if today would be the day I died. I knew the risk. And that made it all the worse.

Hey, hey Dad, what do you think about your son now?

Why would such a smart guy do this? Why would someone like me give up my soul and dance with the devil?

Here I was, while my employees were working hard at my shops. My friends were at their desks, and my wife was at the hospital, helping sick people. I was greeting the day with hard liquor and powder.

Now upstairs in my bedroom with the door locked and fortified with a desk or weights, with a bottle and my bag, I would sit there for hours and hours. I'd pray my phone didn't ring. I'd pray no one wondered where I was. I'd pray no one rang the doorbell. I had contingency plans for all these, but hoped I never had to use them.

None of those plans were very good, though. I had thoughts circulating in my head of being raided by the police. I visualized being caught by my friends and loved ones. In either scenario, I was fucked! I was just going to admit it. That was my plan. I think it's fair to say that part of me wanted to get caught.

The fun never lasted. Fifteen minutes in, and anger would form. So mad at myself! But now I'd gone too far to stop. Now the only thing to do was to numb myself even more. The amount of cocaine I'd consume was disgusting. It was nothing for me to go through an eight ball (about 3.5 grams). Many times it would be more. I don't know how much that is from a legal toxicity level, but I do know that it was what a handful of people would consume in a night at one of my parties. I could go through it in a matter of a few hours by myself.

Then I'd get even more pissed: shaking and shivering, my heart ready to explode. Each new hit did nothing to add to the fun; it just gave me a worse feeling. I just couldn't stop. The romantic feeling was long gone. My paranoia was suffocating, and my day was a complete waste.

Time stood still and yet the whole day disappeared with that first snort.

When Jen was working the seven-to-seven shifts at the hospital, I'd make sure to be done by seven. Around five o'clock I would drink, sometimes an entire bottle of anything with a high alcohol content, to sober up. The liquor would act as a depressant, bringing me down from the high of the cocaine. I was usually so amped up that I could barely control the shaking in my hand.

Some of the nights before Jen got home I'd meet Brian and Andy at a little bar on campus. We went there because not a lot of people were there at 5:00 p.m. on a weekday. The three of us loved to play video golf. I'd meet them after they both had had a productive day at work. They had no clue what I had been doing the last eight hours.

I remember being so careful to not show any signs of my habit. One of the surest ways was to drink. Drinking a lot— that's how I sobered up.

I remember the little bathroom at the Illini Inn. I'd casually, but in a complete state of paranoia, walk into that bathroom and puke my ass off. Then I'd splash water on my face and casually walk out as if nothing had happened. I'd do this every thirty minutes or so until the withdrawal symptoms calmed down. The sobering routine was a ritual as well.

Coming down was rough. Most of the time when I was in there throwing up, nothing came out. I just felt so sick. The shaking and the chills were real. I couldn't believe I had gotten to this point. I'd look in the mirror for what seemed like a hundred times to make sure no clues of drugs were on my nose. I will never forget how hard those first few hours after a binge were. Coming down was hard enough, but hiding it was even harder.

Eventually the booze kicked in. I would get so drunk I would no longer feel the paranoia and the shaking. Sadly, getting completely wasted felt great *because* it got rid of the paranoia and shaking.

I would repeat this several times a week, maybe every other day. What started out as something social was now something entirely different. In fact, I almost never used cocaine socially anymore. It became something I did alone. That's when I knew I had a real problem. I was lost, confused, embarrassed, and terrified.

I was now living a lie. Two lives for one person: Dr. Jekyll and Mr. Hyde.

I'd follow awful days with a good day or two of recovery. My main drive to recover was my feeling of guilt. I had to make it right. I rarely, early on, craved using the next day. I craved making amends for the previous day.

I'd go to the office as if nothing had happened and work my ass off. I'd spend time with my wife as if nothing had happened. I'd stay away from the ritual until I felt like I deserved it again. Or long enough so that I could justify it, or until the withdrawal symptoms were unbearable.

Part of the reason I spaced out these days was to help protect the secret. If I missed too many days in a row, someone was bound to get suspicious. It was a sad secret. I knew it wasn't right. And I thought I could fix it before anyone found out. I just didn't know how or when this would be.

Those off days in between were also how I temporarily built back some self-respect.

When I wasn't boarded up in my fortress going through my ritual, I'd be "on": I was an excellent Jekyll at work and with friends. The bouncing back and forth was no big deal. It wasn't that difficult to juggle. I was excellent at managing my split personality.

It wasn't necessarily that difficult at first to live these different lives, but it was exhausting. I hated what was going on. I was so ashamed. The shame was powerful.

I'm better than this, I thought to myself. People told me I was a good person and it made living in this lie that much more difficult. I couldn't stand the lie.

The only positive I could focus on was the fact that I was a fixer. *I'm gonna fix this*, I'd tell myself. This messy addiction wasn't any different from getting straight A's after getting kicked out of school, and I had made it through then. I'd done this in business, too. Numerous times the company was in a bad way, but in each case somehow I'd turn it all around. I believed I could get myself out of any situation or any mess I created if I absolutely had to! I had history on my side.

One of the best Depeche Mode songs ever is "Walking in My Shoes." I listened to it so much I had it memorized. I connected with this song deeply. I'm not sure if my interpretation is the intended one, but I didn't care.

I would tell you about the things they put me through
The pain I've been subjected to
But the Lord himself would blush
The countless feasts laid at my feet
Forbidden fruits for me to eat
But I think your pulse would start to rush
Now I'm not looking for absolution
Forgiveness for the things I do
But before you come to any conclusions
Try walking in my shoes
Try walking in my shoes
You'll stumble in my footsteps

But this was different. It wasn't just a matter of me working harder. It wasn't just a matter of me igniting my competitive fire. It wasn't just a matter of me hating being a third-world immigrant in a white world and willing myself to achieve and be liked.

I was hooked on a chemical. This was the first time I remember feeling outmatched. Deep down, this was the first time I wasn't sure that I *could* fix it.

CHAPTER 20

Dr. Jeckel and Mr. Hyde, Part II

I *was* good at fixing things. Actually, digging myself out of holes was my specialty. I don't know if it was street smarts, sheer willpower, or having no other choice, but backing myself out of tight corners was what I did best. I managed well when I was desperate. I'd done it all my life.

But as I reflect on that life, I see that it was almost as though I couldn't just succeed at things outright. I couldn't play tennis well for the sake of it—I got really good at it so someone would pay attention to and admire me. I didn't work two part-time jobs to save money to buy the stereo I wanted—I did it because I bitterly resented my parents' poverty and indifference. I needed to hit bottom in each instance in order to motivate me to achieve.

And I was living that horrible cycle again, this time at lightning speed. One day I was a complete, drugged-out mess: Mr. Hyde. The next I was a responsible husband, friend, and boss: Dr. Jekyll.

In some way, knowing I *could* "fix things" gave me a false

sense of security. *See? I can be sober for two days, three days, even four days.* That gave me a confidence that, ironically, made me unafraid of hitting the bottom.

I want to be clear, however, that this "fix-it" strategy was not something I consciously mapped out. I never planned, consciously, to get myself into a bind and then work myself out of it. I always felt that I was trying my best. This up-and-down cycle just sort of happened without me being aware of it until much later. It was only after a decade of therapy that I understood the underlying issues that shaped these patterns.

In addition, my underlying desensitization to feeling disappointment was helpful. Life was too short, I told myself, and so I didn't take it seriously enough to care. I pushed the limits with this mantra as a guiding force. This was partly my own rationalization and partly because it was true.

At the exact time that the drug addition was taking control of my life, so was the need to win: two opposing forces battling daily. I balanced them for years. Destruction followed by achievement followed by destruction followed by . . .

The other "me," the nondestructive "me," needed to win. Winning, to me, was doing the right thing: being a good husband, friend, and boss.

Being a great husband meant not only providing financially for my family but providing them with love and support as well. Being a great friend meant being loyal and positive while bringing as much fun to my friends' lives as I was capable of creating. Being a great boss, a leader, meant doing whatever was necessary to provide long-term security for my employees in a pleasant and fulfilling work environment.

These were things that I was "supposed" to accomplish, based on the talents that I knew I had. I held myself to a high standard in all arenas. I obsessed about how I was doing. I measured my self-worth by my performance. I put a lot of pressure on myself.

Winning meant admiration and respect. I confused admiration with love. All humans need to feel loved, but I didn't know how to discriminate between love and admiration. For me, they were one and the same. Having the respect of my loved ones and friends was monumental.

When I was around people, even though the single most important thing to me was being liked, I never faked my love for them. I genuinely loved people and gave them my best. The tragedy is that I had real love from a lot of people close to me, but I couldn't distinguish between their real love and their admiration for my achievements.

And the greater tragedy was that despite all the love being directed at me, something I so desperately wanted, I was less than genuine with the people I cared so much about. My secret was taking a toll on everything.

Jen and I had a beautiful wedding in two parts. First we got married in a Methodist church, with the white gown and everything. Then we had a traditional Persian ceremony. My friends— all Americans—loved it. They'd never been to anything like that before. Our wedding seemed more like two cultures coming together rather than just two people getting married.

After getting married, Jen and I lived at the Club P house for a few years. It was a terrible time for me and a worse one for my new bride. She hadn't signed up for the double lives I was leading. And she didn't really know what was going on.

This guy she married after dating for only a few months was probably an enigma to her. We didn't have conversations about my odd behaviors (which I describe a little farther on). In some ways I think she was so confused that it may have paralyzed her to address it or confront me. I knew she was loyal, and she wasn't a quitter. Sadly, knowing these traits of hers was in some way part of my calculus.

But I had clues that she was stressed and worried. I would see her cry once in a while. She didn't see me seeing this. Every time I'd see it, I would just tell myself that I would fix it before it got out of hand.

I remember vividly one day coming home and seeing a plate with my license on it lying on the counter. It was the plate from the previous night that I had used to roll up the lines. I had put the contraband under the couch in the living room.

Jen never said a word about it. For a second that gesture reminded me of my mother. Passive aggressive. Did I marry my mom? Maybe I should have been happy that I found someone like my mom. It meant I wouldn't have to have a real conversation.

Later I learned that, because Jen had never seen cocaine, finding the plate and license didn't register for her. She had never touched drugs. It took a long time before she began to be suspicious about my behaviors or the empty Baggies she would sometimes find around the house.

Looking back, it seems impossible that I kept it secret for as long as I did. I had all kinds of techniques I would use to explain my long absences or lengthy trips to the bathroom. One of the tactics I used to keep up the charade was convincing people that I had a "pooping problem." Really.

This "problem" allowed me to take bathroom breaks that lasted hours and were then followed by a few more hours of taking a shower. Somehow this was less embarrassing than my real problem.

When I needed to be medicated and Jen was home and not working, I'd dream up creative ways to spend time in the bathroom. I would start in the bathroom in the morning for a few hours. I would finally emerge, drink a bunch of booze to sober up, and then go mow the lawn.

I can remember sitting on my riding mower, sweating and shaking profusely—counting down the seconds until the last piece of grass was mowed. I'd rub grass and dirt all over myself—a reason for taking a lengthy shower—which would buy me more time in the bathroom. Shower after shower.

It worked. At least it seemed like it did. Now I was back in the bathroom for another few hours. In total, I managed to get six or seven hours in the bathroom, which is about the time I needed to carry out the minimum version of my ritual. I would never have come out if I didn't need to. The only reason I did was to maintain the secret, the illusion.

Brian and Andy started noticing a stain on my right finger, created from me sitting in the shower for so many hours a week with a cigarette attached to my right hand. The stain was so ingrained that I couldn't scrub it out. My buddies even named it: "stanky finger." Because they had written it off as a joke instead of condemning me, my secret seemed safe. So I pushed it and continued.

I remember during 9/11 staying up all night watching the news. Not really, though. I just used that as an excuse.

It seemed to work. When I wasn't in the bathroom I was in the living room watching TV.

As time went on, I had to find more and more creative ways to feed my addiction without getting caught. I would set up meetings out of town. For example, I sometimes went to St. Louis on a trip I made up to meet with auto dealers in my field. I'd drive all the way to St. Louis, but no one was there to meet me on the other end.

I would check into a hotel for a couple of nights. Beforehand I would buy enough supplies to last a normal person weeks. All the supplies I needed, perfectly and methodically packed in my bag. Just the right amount of medicine to last me a few days.

These hotel rituals were particularly scary. I would be in that room for forty-eight hours straight, instead of my normal ten to twelve hours of bingeing. Completely out of my mind, with no responsibilities to my wife, friends, or work to rein me in.

As usual, I would be giddy as I prepared everything and took my first hit. Then it was forty-eight hours of hell. St. Louis, Kansas City, Indy. Same ritual, different Holiday Inn! I would get so messed up that I was sure each one of these retreats was my last. I was sure that one of these days I would not return home.

I would get so worked up. The combination of being awake for days at a time and the amount of drugs I had ingested left me hallucinating.

The weekend would be filled with hours of throwing up, hours of standing with my ear pressed against the hotel door, listening for someone trying to come in. Hours pinned against the window listening for a team of people to come in and find me. Any noise was evidence enough to convince me that I had been discovered and that "they" were coming. I remember one time I heard a helicopter and was convinced it was hovering outside my window with a SWAT team ready to break in.

I would get so worked up. The combination of being awake for days at a time and the amount of drugs I had ingested left me hallucinating. Any noise I'd hear was the evidence to convince me that I had been caught and that I would be discovered.

Hey, hey dad, what do you think about your son now?

The idea of being discovered tormented me. What would I say if my wife, my friends, my employees, who all respected me so much, knew about my ritual? And maybe, most importantly, my dad? They'd know I was a fraud. He'd know I was a fraud. I could imagine the shame. That would be unbearable.

At some point on these fake trips I'd run out of the drugs and booze and come to the realization that I had to end this binge.

The next twenty or so hours would be spent sitting in a dark room: no TV or lights on that would signal my presence. I'd stare for hours at a light fixture in the hotel, telling myself to sleep. Begging my mind and body to rest. Many times I didn't sleep at all.

I would measure my pulse and find the rate terrifying. My heart was beating at an elevated pace for literally thirty hours or so and all I wanted was to sleep. I needed to sleep, and it was impossible.

So I would lie down in my paranoid state for hours, hoping

to miraculously fall asleep or sober up enough to get on the road and head home. I would count from 1 to 100 and then back again. Anything to take my mind off the pounding in my chest and the guilt.

I'd even put on decent clothes. I did this in the event that if I died, I wanted to look proper when I was found.

Finally, it would all come to an end. I'd have to deal with an unbelievable headache. My brain felt like it was banging against the walls of my skull. Over and over . . . no amount of Advil was a match for this headache. I never ate any food during my hotel stays, but I couldn't have eaten anyway.

And then I'd come home.

Once home, Dr. Jekyll appeared. I would go about the house, my office, as if nothing had happened. I'd be engaging, thoughtful, and full of positive energy. I'd feel so sick from what I had afflicted on my body, physically and mentally, and now I had to "Hyde" it.

The stress of hiding my physical discomforts was more difficult than anything I've ever had to do. I would be awake for two to three days straight and then go to work and pretend I was just fine. Keeping up this false image was perhaps the most challenging thing I had ever done. But I did it well. I had to. I kept thinking: *I will fix this. I'll stop soon.*

The horrible thing is that I had acclimated myself to this cycle. As painful and shameful as it was, it was something that I was adapting to and, sadly, something I was actually good at.

I could adapt to anything, given enough time. For example, when I lived in that little apartment across from Centennial High in Champaign, I had a shower leak in the middle of winter. I had no hot water. I took showers in February without hot water, but in my mind, that was the equivalent of getting used to the many moves I had experienced as a kid. It was the equivalent of getting used to going into the poolside mechanical room with my cousin. When bad things happen, you tolerate them. Cold showers, new homes, mechanical rooms—it was all part of the same cycle.

So, this was my life. I juggled the addiction with lies and deceit. Even if I was growing used to the cycle, it was still stressful. Many times, I wished that I would just die.

As time went on, it became more and more difficult to hide this. As you can imagine, with my focus divided, my business was suffering. I could sense and feel that my wife was suffering as well. Even though she didn't have the exposure or experience to know what I was doing, she started to feel something was off. Her sixth sense for my issues was grounded in her childhood. Her father had also struggled with addiction.

I hated this and wanted her to feel safe, but my actions didn't match my thoughts. I was getting sloppy. I was juggling knives and a beautiful glass vase at the same time. I was either going to stab myself with the knife or shatter that precious vase.

CHAPTER 21

The Bottom's . . . Up

I lift my head an inch and turn it to the side. I slowly open one of my eyes and then the other. My vision is foggy, like the fog you see blanketing a harbor early in the morning, gray and dense. My sight and mind are equally foggy. I'm completely disoriented. Not sure where I am or what is going on.

Then I see her as my vision works through this distorted and foggy image. It's my wife. She's just standing there. She's just standing there staring at me. Not a single word. Not one syllable uttered from her mouth. I'm struggling to figure out what's going on.

I lift my head just a tad more and notice a brown cabinet. It looks familiar. I'm trying to piece everything together as fast as I can while she just continues to stand there and stare. Complete silence. It's like she's watching an experiment. She's looking at me like you might study an animal in the zoo, watching its behaviors. I wish I knew what was happening . . .

I'm freezing my ass off. That's another clue I add to the

puzzle. I'm lying down. It's a hard surface, and I'm not comfortable. A tight space!

As I slowly come to, I begin to understand . . . exactly what's going on. I know where I am now. I'm in my Man Room. I'm in my new house. In my basement. It's 2005.

Above me to my right I see a familiar face: a six-inch Scarface doll in a frame that's up on the wall. He's holding a pile of cash in one hand and a semi-automatic in the other. It's all coming back to me. It was one of those nights. I threw another party last nigh, but I only invited myself. Another shameful night! Another night of performing my ritual.

Sadly, this wasn't the first time Jen had seen me like this, but this was the first time I had seen her like this. The look on her face . . . holy shit. I will never forget it.

I saw fear. I saw panic. I saw disappointment. I saw pure sadness. The sadness on her face and in her eyes hurt the worst.

Why isn't she saying anything? Why am I so cold?

As I gather myself, I start seeing what she's seeing. I'm naked. Completely naked! I must have fallen asleep that way. And I'm so uncomfortable, so stiff. I'm not on the couch where I normally end up passing out. I'm lying on the bar.

That's where I slept the night before? Shit! I don't remember a thing. I don't remember climbing onto the bar and I certainly don't remember taking my clothes off. And what I saw next made my stomach clench.

I look toward the floor and all I see is glass. Glass everywhere. As I work through the fog my eyes fixate on this image. An image burned in my memory forever. A bottle of Jack Daniels. A big-boy-size bottle. It's completely destroyed except for the bottom third of the bottle. The bottom of the bottle was sitting up perfectly.

The top, however, looks like a one-inch sword, and it's right in front of my face. I was sleeping inches away from a world of pain, inches away from rolling right onto a minefield of glass shards. I don't know what to say. I usually think well on my feet but . . .

For the life of me, I can't figure out how I ended up naked on my bar. And for the life of me, I can't remember what I said to Jen in that moment. Did she and I even have a conversation? Did I speak at all? To this day, I have never asked or wanted to know. We never talked about it again.

It didn't matter whether or not we had a conversation. It was inconsequential compared to the few words she uttered before walking away.

"I thought you were dead."

I don't have the words to describe the way I felt while I was lying on that bar. No words can describe my heartbreak. No words can describe my disappointment in myself.

I want to scream. I need to scream! I need to cry and I can't. I want to hurt myself. I didn't want to die; I just wanted to physically punish myself. But I didn't do any of those things.

I slowly sat up and looked for a safe landing spot on the glass-covered tile. I worked my way to the side of the bar. Below it there was carpet, where it was safe. I just stared at the ground in disbelief.

I remember that scene like it happened yesterday. It's an image I often think about today. I stayed there and stared at the floor for hours. My mind was racing. A million thoughts were going through my head.

One thought that just kept looping through my brain was, "What if?" What if, instead of Jen seeing me like this, it was our young daughter?

And the one that cut deepest was, "What if she saw me like this—except without a pulse?"

Here I am in my thirties. Married with a child. A businessman. A man of the community. A good friend to a great many. Completely out of control.

The yo-yo existence I was living was taking its toll on just about everything in my life. What happened that day in the basement wasn't really unusual. The only thing unusual was my sleeping naked on my bar surrounded by a halo of glass.

This new level was fueled by the addition of six, seven, or eight painkillers and sleeping pills mixed into my ritual so I could function better after bingeing. It knocked me out, reducing the length of my binges and helping me sleep. I would do a line and immediately start popping pills.

There was clearly a pattern, up and down, only the downs were becoming more and more the dominant force. Even that night on the bar and being found by Jen didn't have enough power to change my behavior and shift me into a different direction.

Afterward, I quit my ritual only for maybe a few days. That's it. In short order, denial and excuses would build a case and the down would have the upper hand on the up. Back to business.

I can't count or remember how many times this cycle repeated itself. The only thing I do know is that it went on for years . . .

One of my dear friends, Adam, asked me to meet him for

lunch. I'd known Adam since high school. I respected the hell out of him. He had excellent judgment. Whatever advice he gave always came from an honest and trustworthy place.

We went to campus to try a new burger place called Junior's. He started by asking how I was. I happened to be in the midst of a bad run, but of course I lied and said I was doing great. In fact, I was in the middle of one of my worst disconnections. I was really out there. This was getting really bad. I was not even that fix-it guy anymore. I was just broken.

He proceeded to tell me about what was going on with my roommates: that is, the people I was sharing a house with: namely, my wife and daughter. Jen had gone to his house the night before or something. Apparently it was serious.

I didn't really listen to Adam like I should have. All I heard were a few key words like "crying" and "moving out." Words Jen had said the night before at Adam and Audrey's house.

I hated to know that she had been crying. I think she had been crying a lot for a long time. Denial is a powerful thing. It definitely protected me, but my denial was slowly breaking the will of the woman who truly loved me in the way that I'd always dreamed of.

So the day finally came. The inevitable. I remember the night, not long after my lunch with Adam. She was sitting in our living room. I was standing in the dining room. My little girl was asleep in her crib. And tears. Not my tears, tears in Jen's eyes.

I didn't feel much at that moment except maybe a little anger. I thought this was extreme, unnecessary, and expensive.

So I went to an extended-stay hotel. It had a little kitchen. In a terrible way I found pleasure in the whole situation. I felt like a college kid again living in an apartment. I stocked the fridge with the stuff I used to eat when I lived alone.

The first night was not so bad. I turned on the TV and got in bed with a few things that could act like a substitute for my medicine. It wasn't always drugs. Sometimes I used food.

That first night away from Jen I lay in bed with a gallon jug of chocolate milk in one hand and a box of Oreo cookies in the other. I ate the whole box. And I drank the whole carton. I effectively put myself into a food coma, a different way of shutting off any ability to feel. Just what the doctor ordered.

Superficially, I looked at it this way: it didn't take me long to get used to life in America when I first moved from Iran. It didn't take me long to get used to a new place each time we moved in Illinois. It certainly didn't take me long to get used to cold showers in February. So why would the transition to living in the extended stay hotel, separated from my wife and baby daughter, be any different?

And it wasn't. Two days into this new existence, I was back in lockdown mode. The doors were locked and barricaded. The chain on the door was engaged, with a chair jammed up against the handle. Here we go again. One snort and I would ungracefully fly myself to the motherland.

CHAPTER 22

No, Thank You!

I had made the call and scheduled an appointment.

The office was small. I filled out some papers for the doctor's receptionist and waited. I didn't really know what to expect. It didn't matter anyway; I was mainly there for show. Going to this appointment would appease my wife and friends, at least for a little while. Just another tactic in my overall strategy to see this addiction through for as long as I could. I wanted it all.

I wanted everyone to leave me the fuck alone. Let me show you my great genius. I wanted them to see the Houdini in me operating at his best. Watch me balance a few thousand-dollars-a-week drug habit with that other person who shared a body with me. The one who was—most times—a great husband, dad, friend, boss, and community leader. It wasn't easy juggling those two selves, but nothing great comes easy.

I was never comfortable being comfortable: If my life wasn't filled with challenges and conflict, it felt far too ordinary. I wanted nothing to do with ordinary. Can you imagine going to work and being consistent and focused? Then coming home and being a good husband and dad? Then calling your parents and brother and talking about what our day had been like? Then getting a good night's sleep, and doing it all over again the next day?

No thank you. That kind of stability was terrifying to me. For me, an unstable existence was stability.

I was clearly sick.

Going to counseling was a bounce-back ploy. I was in fixing mode. I had nothing to lose. At best I would get cured, and at worst I would buy some time. No losing there.

At this point, very few people knew of my issues with substance abuse. It was still a secret that I vigorously kept locked up. Denial was so powerful. The only people who knew I had a problem were my wife and a few close friends, but even fewer knew the extent of it. Being kicked out of the house and being able to return was contingent on me making serious changes.

Part of those changes meant getting help. That's how I heard about Jeckel. Brian knew of him through his business partner's mom and recommended him.

This wasn't my first time going to counseling. I went briefly when I was living at Club P. Jen had insisted I see someone. I'm not sure I totally remember why. But, she thought I needed help, so I went.

The therapist was a nice person, but I was clearly smarter than her and got nothing out of it. I was manipulative and felt in control of the sessions. I went a few times and got pills: antidepressants. Wow, apparently I was depressed. Sure didn't feel depressed. I was having a rip-roaring time.

So here I am sitting with this new guy, an MD. Dr. Jeckel. What a name, huh?

The room was small: maybe 200 square feet at most. A few paintings hung on the walls, and the bookshelf was filled with books that all referenced psychoanalysis.

Jeckel's desk and chair were in the corner. A small coffee table separated him from one other chair. A couch was positioned right next to his chair but facing away from it. You had a choice: the couch or the chair.

I obviously took the chair. No fucking way was I lying down on the couch next to a man—a strange man at that. I couldn't understand why anyone would. If you chose the couch you couldn't even see him or keep an eye on him. I would never, *ever* put myself in that position.

After we go through a quick introduction and small talk, he asks me, "Why are you here?"

What I remember is that before I answered I became aware of the smell of hazelnut coffee. Jeckel had a cup of coffee in his hand, and I wanted one. So I asked for a cup of coffee. He looked at me like I was crazy and politely said, "No."

I didn't get it. *What an asshole*, I thought.

That request for coffee might seem insignificant and harmless, but I know now that it wasn't. Jeckel and I joke about it to this day. That small request—"you have something and I want it, so give it to me now"—was symbolic of my narcissism and the fact that my perception of social situations was off. I had a warped view of what I could take and what was owed to me.

"I need to quit drugs."

He calmly replied, "Why not go to rehab?" He even added, specifically, "Why not got to Hazelton?"

I remember this so vividly. "It's not an option," I said.

And it wasn't. To me, going to rehab would put my secret at risk. Everyone would know. No, thank you!

There was a second reason why rehab wasn't an option. I wanted to keep this party going, but I also really wanted to find the great man that was trapped somewhere in this body amid the addiction and struggles and multiple selves.

It was a battle. I never believed, even then, that the fix for me was going to be a quick one.

I started going to therapy twice a week, even though I really hated being there. Jeckel never gave me advice. What the hell kind of doctor doesn't give advice?

Even worse, if I didn't talk, there would be complete silence. I hated silence. I hated that I hated silence even more. If I was around people and it grew silent, within just a few seconds I would get nervous and my auto-response was to begin talking just to talk. I hated this about myself.

In therapy, in that little room, the silence tormented me. I rambled just to avoid the deafening silence. Jeckel just sat there and listened, rarely offering an opinion.

I wanted to be scolded. I wanted him to tell me what a monster I was. I wanted him to tell me how horrible and irresponsible I was to my family and friends. I wanted him to judge me. I wanted him to guilt-trip me into correcting my behaviors. I wanted him to offer some advice on how to quit. I wanted him to give me tricks to avoid the need to use.

There was none of that. Just silence. He just listened. And

what was worse, he empathized and understood. Being genuinely listened to . . . that was the worst of all.

I kept going to my appointments. I told him everything. I told him about Iran, Gurnee, California, and even my cousin. I told him about Iranian culture. I made him watch a movie, *The House of Sand and Fog,* about the challenges, humiliation, and pain immigrants from Iran felt once they fled Iran.

I wanted him to watch this powerful movie and gain insight into me. And I wanted to see whether or not he'd really watch it. Did he care enough about me to take the time to do this? By doing so, he would show me he was serious about fixing my illness.

He watched the movie within a few days of me giving him the DVD.

We were six months into working together in therapy. I was sharing a lot of my life with Jeckel, my history and my thoughts. I was getting very comfortable with him and the process.

That's the precise moment I quit.

I didn't like the feeling of being comfortable. I got paranoid. Jeckel was too good to me. Too understanding and loving. That scared the hell out of me.

Some of the games I played were dreamed up consciously and others were done unconsciously. For example, to punish him, I would schedule sessions and purposely skip them.

I remember standing on my deck one evening when I got a call from Jeckel. *Bizarre,* I thought. *I don't even know him that well and he's calling me after hours?* He wanted to know where I'd been and what was going on. I made up some bullshit excuses and humored him by going back to therapy.

Then the feelings of paranoia happened again, and I thought I knew why, so I started skipping sessions once more, even though I lied to Jen and told her I was still going. I had become convinced that Jeckel had ulterior motives. Was he manipulating me into something I wasn't interested in? Did he have a crush on me? I was sure of it. I had heard about this: stories about the doctor preying on the weak and vulnerable patient. Was that me?

But I was too smart for that and I put an end to it before it could escalate. I would not go down that path—not this time, and never again. *See you later, Jeckel . . . I'll fix my problems by myself. Just like I've done my whole life.* There had always been a reason why I never put myself in a position to depend on anyone. That wouldn't change. I didn't need Jeckel or anyone else to help me.

CHAPTER 23

The ABCs

My dueling lives were taking a toll on everything I touched. Everything I loved. Drip . . . drip . . . drip. A faucet leak that wouldn't quit. Each drip on its own was manageable, but bit by bit the sink began to back up. Finally, it threatened to overflow.

I grew anxious without a fix in sight. One moment I would be lying next to a towel covered with bloodstains from a nose that refused to stop bleeding. The next I was "on" at work or home, winning at everything I touched.

I was the most consistent inconsistent person I knew.

I had been in and out of therapy for a couple of years. Nothing about my life had really changed except that Jen and I had two more children—both girls. When I showed up at therapy, I worked at it. I worked at it really hard. The starts and stops with therapy were, I think, part of the process for me. Or, really, maybe the interruptions were part of the process of me testing Jeckel.

Sitting inside that little room, I formed a love-hate relationship with Jeckel early on. I suppose it's no surprise I lacked trust, especially since I was in a position of vulnerability with him.

I spent a lot of time and energy testing Jeckel. I did this from Day One, and I kept it up for years. He wasn't the only person who went through a period of examination with me.

Most people had to pass my bizarre tests, born from pathological paranoia. The level and scope of the tests depended on what value I placed on the potential of the relationship. If I anticipated the person being someone important to me, the process of testing could go on for years. It was different for every person. It was even different depending on my psychological state and paranoia at the time.

In the case of Jeckel, it was all about his memory. Which, in essence, was about his listening skills. Which, ultimately, had to do with how much he really cared about me. What I did was simply test how well he paid attention to the details of our conversations. As someone who clearly didn't feel listened to as child, knowing that someone was paying attention to my words and my thoughts was critical in gaining my trust.

I wasn't completely neglected as a child. I was listened to, but not for the right reasons—or at least the reasons that I wanted. I was listened to for only one purpose: to make sure my thoughts matched my parents' thoughts. This alignment was critical for them. I believe it satisfied their needs and fears. They were completely unaware of what they were doing or why.

So naturally I quit sharing any of my thoughts with my family. As a young boy, I realized that my thoughts and feelings would be better served locked up in the fat cells of my brain.

In the rare times that my thoughts were expressed, they were judged, scrutinized, and, ultimately, manipulated. God forbid I share an idea that was as an authentic thought of my own and that my parents would listen without their internal bias. That they would listen for my sake, not theirs.

Conversations with my parents went like this:

"You SHOULD think this way . . ."

"You DON'T want that . . ."

"You NEED this . . ."

"You SHOULDN'T feel that way . . ."

That got old, so I quit sharing and kept everything in.

But Jeckel, a doctor who was *supposed* to give me advice, didn't do anything like that. He didn't tell me what I should feel or what I needed or how I should think. He just listened. This made me very suspicious at first.

Even worse than simply listening, he did something that made me even more suspicious and paranoid: he never judged. Never. No matter what I told him. This response—or lack of it—threw me off entirely.

What's he up to? I would think. It was unfamiliar territory for me, so I kept my defenses up. The armor I wore was quite fortified. Without any other options, I amped up the testing. I was relentless. It went on for a long time.

I wish I were a better chess player. I'm decent, but I should be better. I have always been a good strategist, in both business and life, especially back then. But my ability to strategize made me a bit manipulative, and I didn't love this about myself.

In chess you move a pawn and place it in a certain formation somewhere on the board in hopes that your opponent sees what you wanted them to see. But the magic is in the set of moves they don't see. Smoke and mirrors.

My ability to create smoke and mirrors is what made me successful. On a daily basis, it's what helped me get by. Ironically, it also contributed to my dislike of myself, because it made me feel less than genuine. Remember, I hate fake people, including myself at times.

Like a Russian chess player, I set up moves and waited patiently until my prey fell into the trap. With Jeckel, I manipulated a conversation about a chosen topic. I would leave little nuggets of detail in those conversations. As I spoke, I would note his reaction: his facial expression, words, and movements. I'd burn those reactions into my memory.

Then, weeks later, I'd bring up the same chosen topic, except I would modify the structure of the conversation. Use a slightly different context, enough to disguise it. Then I'd listen and take note. I was looking for only one thing: I wanted to see the same reactions from Jeckel no matter what context I brought up the conversation in. I didn't want someone who was lazy, rehearsed, and chose the path of least resistance.

Why? Because if he was listening deeply, it would mean he genuinely cared about me. I wanted that so badly, not just from him, but from everyone. I hated liars and fakes.

These tests that I dreamed up, for Jeckel and for others, made it tough on folks. It also made it tough on me. I hated the sick levels of paranoia and the amount of energy I spent searching for unconditional love, for authentic and real relationships. My guinea pigs didn't know they were part of an experiment born from my paranoia and insecurity when it came to relationships. But they were. Everyone was subject to these tests. It was my reality.

The standards I held people to were perhaps unattainable and clearly stemmed from my illness. In reality, I wanted everyone to fail. I continually searched for evidence that supported an underlying belief that I had subscribed to for most of my life: most people are not *real* or *honest*. Furthermore, most people are inherently *selfish*. And finally, everyone has ulterior motives.

Anyone who liked me fell under all my dreamed-up suspicions. My first thought was *Why on earth would they like me?* because, deep down, *I* didn't like me. Then, if they maintained that façade, I'd wonder what they wanted.

This paranoia was even more magnified in therapy because I was paying my doctor for his assistance and help. No patients, no money. I assumed that for Jeckel our relationship was just a job. He had a mortgage and bills like all of us. Even worse, I made the inaccurate assumption that he had no incentive for me to get well. Wouldn't he be without a job if everyone got well?

Many times throughout the early years I'd show up for long periods of time without having done too much self-reflection or analysis. Then, without any good reason, I'd quit. And then, once again, I'd go back without any consciously derived reason. There was no rhyme or reason to my starts and stops.

When I did show up, I would make progress—at least I thought so as I started trusting Jeckel and started to open up more and more. I was teachable and had a passion for learning more and more about myself. I made my biweekly trips to that little office. I went grudgingly at times, but all that mattered was that I showed up.

Jeckel continued to pass my tests. It was remarkable how genuine his connection was. I had never ever experienced anything like this. I started to share my life and thoughts with him. I even started sharing my dreams with him. Not life dreams, but the dreams you have at night. I was a big dreamer. I remember most of the dreams I have and have always liked to analyze them. With Jeckel I learned how to do it the right way.

We talked a lot about my childhood. I shared in detail everything that I was exposed to in the physical world as a child. I described the moves back and forth from Iran and all the moves in America. And, at my most vulnerable, I told him about the mechanical room by the pool. It was the hardest thing I'd had to do.

What seemed to get Jeckel's attention was not so much the details of the "how" and the "what" of what happened, but my feelings at the time. He wanted to know how I felt when the event happened to me as a boy and also how I felt talking about the event as a grown man.

We also spent a lot of time talking about relationships within my family. Jeckel was very curious about my father and mother and each one's psyche. Who were my parents? How had they evolved into their current state? He was curious about my brother too. What was he was like? Who was he? What did my family talk about? What did we share with one another?

Jeckel was trying to drill down on how I was raised and nurtured psychologically. He knew I was injured by certain events, but I could tell early on that he was more interested in the psychological trauma of our family dynamics, not material world trauma like the moves and my cousin: in other words, the injuries that came as a result of the style of parenting I was raised under.

He had my parents pegged early. There wasn't much that surprised him. He, like me, knew their negative behaviors weren't malicious. My parents were not mean or purposely abusive. For example, whenever my mom would see me or even my friends, it would take merely three seconds before she would start commenting on their appearance and weight. Harmless, right?

Well, even though my parents meant no harm, their attention to my physical appearance (and my brother's) did hurt. This was partially their habit, but it was cultural as well. Vanity is significant in Iranian culture. I'm sure it was even magnified in my immigrant parents, visitors in this new "white" world called America.

My parents had their own childhood injuries that made them limited. Throw in the fact that they also got a rug pulled out from under their world. Fleeing from their homeland against their will with two young children wasn't an easy thing to become reconciled to. And, as if that wasn't enough, add the fact that they did not speak the same language as my brother and me. I mean that literally. We had a huge communication gap. My father and mother really didn't try hard to be American. I can't imagine having to leave your country only to start all over again. I worked hard to be able to put myself in their shoes.

I believe now and have always believed that they didn't assimilate because they clung to a fantasy in which they would go back to Iran and pick up exactly where they had left off. To this day they don't speak anything but Farsi unless they have to, and all their friends are Iranian.

Despite the things I knew I hated about my parents' behaviors, I didn't feel like my upbringing was anything exceptional. Nothing I had endured was that incredible. Jeckel had to convince me that being abused or being uprooted without any notice, conversation, or reassurance was a tad unusual. I had my own denial about this that I needed to work through.

I thought many kids endure and are exposed to things that are unthinkable: far worse than anything most of us can relate to—far worse than anything I'd had to go through. There are also many kids who endure great horrors and yet are remarkably healthy later in life. Their ability to flourish, I learned, was a function of their "core" strength. A function of the foundation that their psychological nurturing was built on. I didn't have this core.

That foundation is created from unconditional love and strong mirroring early in your childhood. Mirroring is the key. Children need to see themselves in a mirror that truly reflects who they are rather than the needs and fears of their caregivers.

Tragedy occurs when you face challenging events but have a poor internal structure to handle adversity: a weak and unmirrored core.

So, my foundation was weak. As a child, I didn't have any understanding of the fact that my lack of emotional tools wasn't my fault. My parents were limited and suffering as well. Obviously, as a child I couldn't process this. I wasn't able to account for their behavior toward me, and I also didn't have my own functioning emotional toolbox from which to draw the proper tactics to cope. So, I got angry. I got frustrated. I just wanted to be heard, but it was like my parents were emotionally deaf.

In my sessions with Jeckel we talked a lot about these events and their emotional affect on me. I remember clearly what he wanted. He wanted me to say it. He wanted me to scream and say how much I hated it. He wanted me to mourn. He wanted me to scream and say how much it broke my heart and how unfair it all was. But it was very difficult for me. I was so protective of my parents.

He wanted to me say those words because I was clearly in denial. He wanted me to know it was okay to be mad at my parents, to be sad about their emotionally neglecting me. Yet, even though I was angry, I remained protective of their needs, which I confused with their happiness. I'd sacrifice my own well-being, both in therapy and in real life, to maintain this image I had of them.

Those words and thoughts were hard for me. I fantasized and dreamed of a day when, miraculously, my dreams of a perfect family would become a reality. To me a perfect family meant one thing: I just wanted my parents to *know me* and for me to *know them*.

Never, never, never, never, never! This was a line from Shakespeare's play *King Lear,* which Jeckel always brought up in therapy in our early sessions. I didn't know the story, and I hated to read fiction, so I took his word for it.

He'd say, "You need to know this, Parham: You will *never* have the very thing you so badly yearn for, and until you come to terms with this 'not having,' you will not grow . . ."

And so I would repeat after him: "I will *never, never, never* . . ." I would say but the words, but the next step was to actually believe it, and then eventually to feel it. Saying it and feeling it are two very different things. I needed to mourn my losses. I would need to come to terms with the reality that I would never be able to go back in time. I would *never* have the relationship I wanted. I would *never* have some of the needs I so badly wanted met.

It was critical for me to mourn. To feel the anger and get in touch with what that did to me was part of integrating my multiple selves. It was also important for me to forgive myself, my parents, everyone, and to realize at a very deep level that this is just the way it was. As Jeckel put it: "It's just *so*. This is who you are and why you are!"

It was great having these conversations. And that's all they were at first. I needed to learn the "ABCs" of therapy. Jeckel was very patient. It took me a lot of sessions and time to figure out the nature of this type of therapy, of psychoanalysis. You have to learn the alphabet before you can learn to construct a word.

It was an ordinary session, and I don't remember the topic we were talking about. But I remember the heat I felt in my face. Sitting across from Jeckel, I felt this burning sensation all over my face. I felt as if I had been instantly struck with a fever. All of sudden my hands started to shake for no reason. My teeth and face all clenched.

I turned my head away from Jeckel. I remember feeling ashamed. I looked at everything in that room except him. The paintings, the desk, the books. I remember looking up and fixing my eyes on the white ceiling. I stared without emotion until that strange sensation went away. A few minutes and it was over.

The shaking subsided and my face was back to a more manageable temperature.

Like he often did when he knew something I didn't know, and especially when I went silent, as I did in this case, Jeckel gently asked, "What are you thinking about?"

The sensation was back. I clenched my teeth again and tried to speak and quickly stopped. I turned away from him and turned my mind completely off. That was the furthest I wanted to go in that session. I rang the bell and class was dismissed. I walked out.

Later that day I was in my basement, but this time I was being a good boy. Not in my Man Room, but in my home gym. I was in a clean phase of my life. I was working hard in all aspects of my life, especially therapy.

I was exercising in the basement. "Running" on the elliptical machine, listening to music. Midge Ure's "If I Was," a song that connects me to Gurnee and that awful day in October 1985 when my life as a happy, popular high school freshman was turned upside down.

Like it happened yesterday, I remember the sensation that came over me—similar to what I was feeling in Jeckel's office a few hours earlier. And then the feeling evolved and grew more powerful. Now my legs felt numb and wobbly. Time slowed to a crawl. The elliptical slowed, too. No matter what I did, it moved slower than the force I was applying to it.

I stepped off the elliptical machine and purposefully lowered myself to the floor. I got down on all fours on the carpet. My teeth unwillingly clenched like my life depended on it. I felt the pain . . ."*never, never never*" . . . an unfamiliar feeling . . .

I slowly lowered my face to the carpet, just feet away from the bathroom where I had spent so many hours collapsed on the floor, but for very different reasons. Completely blindsided by this wave of emotion, I lay there for a few minutes. Then, finally, it happened.

It had been twenty-plus years, maybe more, since the last time. Yet I remembered the last time vividly. I was sitting in the front passenger seat of our family's car, a white Buick, outside our house in Gurnee. The house was to my right. It was a Saturday morning. I'm pretty sure it was October 4 or 5, 1985. A sunny fall day. Tears were running down my cheeks, and I heard my dad's voice saying, "You shouldn't cry."

I instantly followed my dad's order and stopped crying. Then I made myself a promise. I would never cry again.

Until . . .

Head down on the ground with my face pressed against the carpet in my basement gym, my body literally shaking, I cried. I mean, I *cried*. I cried in a way I didn't know was possible for a human. I cried for a long time.

It was cathartic. The tears were endless and the cries were loud, more like groans. This cry was powerful. The cry stemmed from a deep part of me; depths I never imagined or knew existed. Hurt I had never felt before. The intensity and magnitude is hard to describe in words. This went on for a long time.

When the last tear finally subsided, I remember thinking, "I'm worn the fuck out!"

I lay there, exhausted, for a long time and tried to analyze the experience. *What the hell just happened?* I wanted to call Jeckel. I wanted to tell Jen. I did neither. I was too embarrassed.

And, strangely, I felt really great. I'm not sure I had ever felt that way. Besides a much-needed purging of repressed feelings, I also felt a great surge of optimism. I saw a light at the end of the tunnel.

I think that cry served as the *single most important* event to date in my long road to recovery. I was now a real believer in the process. I felt a heightened conviction in the process and the direction of this type of therapy. *Maybe it really works,* I thought. I was on my way to mastering my ABCs, and now it was time to turn the newly learned alphabet into words . . .

CHAPTER 24

Mirror, Mirror on the Wall . . .

The type of therapy I was doing isn't for everyone. Most people want a quick fix. Most people want a pill or a few nuggets of advice or a few words of wisdom that miraculously change your life. Believe me, if I thought that would work for me, I would have been all-in.

As troubled as I was, a quick fix was not for me. A thirty-day inpatient rehab program or a ten-step program would not have worked for me. Those programs would have potentially stopped me from using external chemicals to medicate myself, but they would have not fixed the underlying cause or defect. In my opinion, stopping using would have been a superficial change.

The drugs, scary as it sounds, were just a symptom of the problem, not the problem itself. I needed to delve beyond the surface. I needed to go deeper if I was ever going to solve this puzzle. And I needed to solve it forever. Psychoanalysis was the only solution that made sense. At least it was the only thing that made sense to me.

Everyone learns and processes information differently. For

new concepts or skills to click for me, I need to understand them on a fundamental level. For example, I was a decent student despite the fact that I dreaded memorization. In math, I couldn't memorize a formula for the life of me until I truly understood how it was constructed. Once I grasped both the theory and the mechanics of what the formula was about, I would never forget it and could properly apply it at a level that was much higher than the one we were being taught.

The same would turn out to be true of my emotional intelligence.

Many times I'd see Jeckel three times a week, once a week at a minimum. Two weekly sessions was usually the right dose.

I perversely saw a certain beauty in this type of therapy. Self-discovery is time-consuming, like peeling an onion by hand, layer by layer. As each layer gets peeled, you find it to be rewarding, painful, and terrifying all at the same time. And, just like with an onion, the more layers you peel, the more you find yourself tearing up.

As Jeckel used to say, psychoanalysis is like "playing with dynamite." He was right. I know several people who have engaged in therapy like this and, for one reason or another, have quit. The emotional risks can be too devastating unless you're committed to seeing the process through. Until you go through the process yourself, you may not understand what I'm talking about.

I told Jeckel my dream early in our relationship. And I wanted him to promise—promise *me*—that if I stuck with him and this type of therapy, my dream would come true.

In my dream, I'm in my fifties. I'm sitting in a European

café. I'm just sitting. I'm not stuffing my face with food or my lungs with nicotine. I look down at my legs and, to my amazement, I notice them resting calmly on the ground. My legs are not bobbing up and down. They are still.

I'm looking around and enjoying the sights and sounds of the city . . . free from anxiety . . . my brain operating in the present. I'm alone and content. My mind doesn't drift to the past, and my mind doesn't drift to the future. I'm not thinking about the *next* thing and I'm not thinking of the *last* thing. I'm just sitting. A sense of peace and calm is flowing through my body and mind. I'm willingly and naturally able to stay in the moment. No fear and no needs.

This is what I wanted Jeckel to promise I could get.

The sessions were not lectures. They were not designed to be "advice" sessions. They were explorations of my past and how that informed my present. They moved slowly and methodically. It took a long time for any progress to be made.

Success in therapy is dependent on two things: (1) a patient's willingness to delve patiently into childhood, and (2) the guidance of a great therapist. I was lucky to have the latter, and I progressively developed the ability to master the former.

I learned a lot in those sessions with Jeckel. I delved into some terrifying memories and experiences. But, strangely, I found myself welcoming the discomfort. Over the years, my desire for and confidence in the process grew to a point where therapy was just part of my daily life. Whether I was physically in that chair or not didn't matter; I was in psychoanalysis 24-7. No day went by without me working on issues, working on my betterment. It was like breathing.

Almost anything I did or thought I analyzed and put into the context of the defects I had uncovered in therapy. A simple example is this: Every time I spoke to anyone, I would analyze why I said the things I said. Did I say it to impress them? Was I listening to the other person, or was I being a narcissist and only paying attention to how this conversation related to me? It was an easy test to run.

This was also the case with any business decisions I made. For instance, at a very simple level, I would think about "why" I made a certain decision. Was it to feed my ego? If so, was I making the choice because I was feeling weak and insecure? If I concluded that was the case, then I would pause and reflect before following through. These are just a few examples of how therapy was with me constantly.

Early in therapy I committed myself to never lying. If I was here to *truly* get better, then I couldn't lie. Jeckel needed the correct info: junk in, junk out. A drug addict gets really good at lying to protect his or her addiction. I was no different. It wasn't hard for me to lie, yet I always thought of myself as an honest man. But I lied a lot, especially to protect my secret.

I didn't lie when I was in Jeckel's little room. It was a safe zone for me. The little room was free from judgment. This fact allowed me to feel comfortable with the truth. Judgment has always been something I despise. I had been on the receiving end of it all my life, so *not* having it was refreshing and productive.

I'd tell Jeckel when I was a bad boy, knowing that he would not inflict any judgment on me. His lack of judgment wasn't an act either, because I would have easily detected that. He knew every time I quit, and he knew every time I fell off the wagon. He knew about every weekend binge and he knew every single line item on my long list of insecurities.

Jeckel respected me as person.

When I started therapy, I thought I'd get diagnosed with some kind of disorder: maybe a cool diagnosis like *attachment disorder*, which affected relationships. It arises from the failure to form attachments with one's primary caregivers in infancy and childhood. The first time I ever heard of this disorder was from a girlfriend. She thought I had it, since I wasn't good at getting attached to people.

Or maybe I would be diagnosed with *bipolar disorder*. That one sounded crazy and complicated—a perfect fit for me. The term "bipolar" was going around like a flu bug. At the time, it was a buzzword for anyone with odd behavior or who was up and down. By definition it was a disorder that was associated with mood swings: one minute you're depressed and the next you're experiencing a manic high.

I was clearly all over the place, so bipolar made perfect sense. I really was hoping that it was my diagnosis (how sick that I thought a mental illness was a cool thing to have). Being bipolar had a certain enigma or sexiness to it.

My radar was sharp when it came to hearing people casually diagnose others or even themselves. It really annoyed me for some reason . . . Anyway, so what was I? Bipolar?

In the early days it was, "What's my problem, Doc?" and "What do I have?"

I have *what*? Depression? No way, I'm not depressed! I'm happy, successful, and well liked. I don't walk around moping.

I have plenty of energy. Yeah, sure, I do lock myself up weekly in a bathroom for twelve hours at a time, and yeah, I do shove a ton of chemicals through my bloodstream most days of the week. But, that aside, I am pretty happy. I didn't know it was a crime to work hard and party hard. Isn't that what life is all about, Doc?

Okay, Jeckel, so if I am, in fact, depressed, when did I catch it?

Maybe I caught it on that train ride escaping Iran? We were packed in there like sardines. Maybe I got it from that fat man wrapped in layer after layer of colorful textiles. I couldn't stop staring at him as I watched him getting beaten by those guards. I must have caught it from him through my stare! Or maybe I caught it in the poolside mechanical room from my cousin. That makes perfect sense. I'm sure some depression germs were transmitted in one of those encounters.

I showed up for each session, my apparent (and disappointing) depression in tow. I talked and Jeckel listened. I was very teachable, but it was still tough to grasp this depression thing.

Ironically, I had been a psychology major in college. I still thought being depressed meant you had to be sad and failing at something. In general, I was grandiose, loud, and confident around people. How could a sad person act that way?

So I just talked, listened, and learned . . . Now let's get weird and deep!

Depression, as I learned, was something entirely different. Depression for me was the result of years of denial and repression. The denial of my *true* and *real* emotions at a very early age.

What the hell does that mean? This is how Jeckel explained it to me.

As children (and, if we aren't properly differentiated, as adults), when we stare into our parents' eyes, we are looking into a mirror. What we see in that mirror defines our entire development. The problem is that the mirrors our parents are holding up are often full of cracks and distortions that have nothing to do with us, and everything to do with our parents' own issues.

So it was with my own parents. When I brought them my thoughts and feelings, I didn't see an authentic little Parham reflected back at me. What I found instead was their expectations of me or their fears they had for me. The Parham my parents reflected back to me wasn't really about me or affirming me as a person. Instead, it was a mechanism for soothing their own anxieties. Rather than seeing me, I saw their projections. But I didn't know enough to know the difference.

Here's a simple example to illustrate my point. Imagine a little boy crying. It doesn't matter why he's crying; maybe it's because he lost a toy. As he's crying, he notices that his mom's reaction is disappointment. She's disappointed in her little boy for not being tough enough, for crying for no good reason. The way the mom is reflecting her son is unconscious; it's all she knows. She's unequipped to understand that she is projecting her fears onto the little boy.

Now imagine this happening over and over. The little boy cries, the mom reacts with disappointment. That little boy will have no choice but to create layers to emotionally insulate himself from that shame he now has about crying.

I understand this because it was my experience as a child. It wasn't malicious. My parents can't have known what they were doing. It takes a lot of effort to nurture a child's emotional development without throwing in your own unfulfilled needs or layering on your own anxieties. This is difficult even for people with sophisticated emotional toolboxes.

Jeckel gently led me down this path, exploring the ways in which the mirror my parents held distorted my image of myself. Although I could understand the idea intellectually, it was hard to take seriously. So what if I wasn't *mirrored properly*? Who is? I spent a lot of energy dismissing Jeckel's theories as well as the implications faulty mirroring had for me.

Ruminating on the cracked mirror seemed horribly critical. But who was I to pick apart my parents' style of parenting? Doing so felt wrong, and I fought with Jeckel about this on a weekly basis. Who was I to be so demanding and ungrateful? My parents had done the best they could through some very difficult times. They had protected my brother and me. They had put food on the table. We were never homeless. They had worked their hardest to make sure their sons were able to go to college, and they built better lives for us while making a lot of sacrifices along the way.

Figuring out the ways their parenting had failed me felt like I was just picking on them. I made sure that Jeckel knew how uncomfortable I was "talking badly" about them. I minimized everything negative in my life anyway, so my relationship with my parents got the same treatment. I defended them. I empathized with their struggle. I had to explain to Jeckel and I had to remind myself that having to flee their country in the midst of a revolution was extremely difficult. That was enough to warrant a pass for their inadequate parenting . . .

And, somehow in the process of justifying their behavior, I forgot that I'd lived the same experiences. Jeckel made sure to remind me of that every time I would minimize my experiences and magnify theirs.

It was years into therapy before this mirroring thing made any sense. When I finally started to accept the idea that our identities are shaped not only in our own heads but also by the reactions of others, it became clear to me that more people than just my parents were holding mirrors. But the distortions in my parents' mirrors had infected my sense of self. This played out in strange ways in the rest of my life. It took going to therapy to understand those repercussions.

I loved big gatherings. (I am sure that comes as no surprise by now.) The bigger the party, the more it mattered to me. The number of guests, the quality of guests, the level of planning— it was all an elaborate game for me. It didn't matter if the party was a fundraiser, a gala, or just a party. (There was no such thing for me.) It was all a game.

The game had a purpose. What looked like someone just having fun was actually a carefully constructed and overanalyzed social experiment. Would I succeed or would I fail?

When I was at one of these parties, I had one of my "selves" running around the room playing Mr. Popular. I was good at socializing and liked it. I could fit myself like a chameleon into any setting and strike up a good conversation with anyone. But Mr. Popular wasn't the only Parham in the room.

The other Parham, my observing ego, was watching from

above. I would analyze the dynamics of the conversation I was in. How was I participating? Was I successful at being charming? It wasn't just me I was watching but the whole dynamics of the room. Who was talking to whom? Who was getting a lot of attention and who wasn't? Who was the most comfortable in their small group and who was branching out and making new conversations? This all mattered to me. I felt like I had a gift in being able to see all this simultaneously.

Even in the middle of a conversation, I would notice from the corner of my eye someone across the room finishing a conversation and then making a beeline toward me. I'd see them coming from all the way across the room. Just to say hi. This happened a lot. It was sickening that I noticed this and I hated myself for caring about it. It gave me a high. The attention was very satisfying.

As the evening progressed, I would work closer and closer to my desired outcome. The win was simple. It was all about attention: how much attention—both qualitative and quantitative—I received. I knew when the target amount was reached because I would simply just feel better. By the end of the night my self-esteem was as high as the clouds.

I always got the win, the "high," if that was my goal.

The attention I got at parties became something I counted on. I did everything in my power to attend or throw parties, to talk to everyone who attended, to find something to connect about, and to add another tally on my scorecard. It sounds malicious, but it wasn't, really. I was a social animal caught in a vicious cycle. I genuinely enjoyed connecting with people; it's just that what was fueling my rampant need for that connection was an underlying psychological injury.

But I lacked any awareness of what was going on.

That awareness came later, with Jeckel. Mirroring—or, really, the lack of positive mirroring in my childhood—was the foundation. I confused admiration (what I received at parties) with real love. Instead of my self-esteem being fueled by self-love or love from others, it was poorly constructed. I needed the *affirmation* that I got in my social encounters to feel good about myself.

My self-esteem was a bubble on the verge of bursting. So I did everything I possibly could to keep the bubble from popping. I sought an endless array of self-esteem substitutes: drugs, popularity, gambling, achievement, winning . . .

The pain came when the party ended. The noise subsided and was no longer around to help me drown out the voices. There went the admiration . . . and the love. I would be at home by myself, without any mirroring. The bubble would begin to tremble. I can remember this happening a thousand times.

That social high should have been enough to carry me, but it wasn't. By the time I was home, I couldn't even look myself in the mirror. I couldn't see what everyone else could see. My mirror was cracked.

When I looked in my mirror, I saw an ugly man. Disgusting at times. An immigrant with brown skin. A hairy Persian! I would look at my face and all I saw was a big head and fat cheeks. I would see a bald head and a forehead full of wrinkles. I might not have understood the nuances of self-esteem, but I knew enough to know I was looking at a deeply insecure boy.

The more therapy I did, the more I hated getting in conversations with people about depression. Everyone thought they knew what depression was, but most people I came across didn't have a clue. Especially the ones that had been to therapy for a short time and therefore thought they "got it."

Years and years into therapy, it could be a very isolating experience. The more I delved, the more I felt I couldn't relate to anyone. Most people don't do this kind of analysis on themselves. Therapy, as I've discussed, teaches you a whole new language of self-examination. Childhood injuries. Mirroring. Depression. Observing egos.

For someone who had so much invested in constantly making connections with people (the very foundation of my self-esteem), this was crushing. In the process of facing myself, I was having to do what I hated most: be lonely. In the depths of that loneliness, I finally felt the depression that had apparently been chasing me my whole life—what Jeckel wanted me to connect to.

Drugs, money, and popularity. Those had been my talismans to ward off the ugly emotional mess inside of me. That toxic concoction created so much noise that I never had to listen to what was really happening with me. I certainly didn't think I had gone to therapy for depression. I would never have diagnosed myself that way.

This isn't unusual. Many successful, seemingly happy people suffer from depression. Part of the reason they keep "the ride" going is that if things ever stop, they are forced to face themselves. They have to feel what is really going on with them. It's a subconscious act. I am still strangely jealous of people who aren't aware of the underlying pain that is fueling their drive. Life is simpler when you are ignorant of your demons, especially when the demon is depression.

Ignorance is bliss; but, for me, it was no longer an option. I had delved too deep. Therapy is like a grenade: Once you blow the pieces of your poorly constructed self-esteem apart, you have to put it back together. If you don't do the work, you will turn to your old, unhealthy coping mechanisms. Your symptoms will end up even worse.

I went to therapy because of the *consequences* of my depression. The destructive whirlwind I'd become to avoid myself was so formidable that I had no choice. I either had to get help or . . . who knows. Maybe die.

The irony is that my raging drug habit, while it caused deep pain, saved my life and, through pushing me into therapy, introduced me to my real self.

CHAPTER 25

'Til Death Do Us Part

I am my harshest critic, especially during the period that I found myself so entangled in the claws of destruction. Reflecting on this period leaves me wondering about so many "whys?".

Why would Jen want to stay married to me?

Why would she want to have kids with me?

Why does Jen love me?

Why does anyone love me?

There was a long list of questions I had both then, in that period of fog, and after . . .

I think I know what Jen saw when we got married. I was educated, successful, loyal, and loving. But she didn't know of the undercurrent of my depression and the extent of it. But then, neither did I.

My depression wore a mask that fooled us all, an insight that I have learned over time.

Back then, the future seemed bright and we wanted to have a family. We wanted to have kids right away. I was thirty when

I got married, so my clock was slightly ticking. She is six years younger, so didn't have the same urgency.

We quickly realized that having children wasn't going to be as easy as we may have thought. And I quickly realized *again* that things just don't seem to come easily for me.

After many attempts to get pregnant, we had to explore scientific intervention. We saw many specialists and went through a very difficult period that culminated in having to go the route of in vitro fertilization, or IVF (baby-making in a culture dish).

It failed the first few times; then, we finally got pregnant. But the excitement was short-lived. We lost the baby after eight weeks. Jen was heartbroken. I had mixed feelings. I was in the beginning stages of elevating my solo partying. As the pressure to have a child mounted, my drug use increased.

Later, Jeckel would explain to me the impact that a child would have had on my fragile psyche, but at the time, I couldn't comprehend this nor did I think my partying was out of my control.

In fact, I was sure that once we finally have a child I would evolve and find the partying dull and unnecessary. I always heard people say things like, "Once I had little Tommy, everything changed." I remember my brother saying how having his first child shifted all the attention from himself to her. I hoped this would prove to be true for me too.

The slippery slope I was on was getting exponentially more slippery by the day. Even Jen knew I was going in the wrong direction, but I believe she, too, subscribed to the same theory that a child would end this cycle and a new healthy pattern would be formed out of sheer responsibility to another being. I think she believed that I would become the person who wasn't going to, metaphorically, blow himself up.

So we kept trying and eventually IVF worked a second time. We made it past several key periods and the odds increased by the week. It was becoming clear that this new baby was going to become a reality. And that's when Jeckel warned me.

I was only a few months or so into therapy. I didn't know the ABCs, so his warning fell on deaf ears. He tried to explain that a needy person like me would have less attention once the baby arrived. Jen's focus would shift to the newborn, and I would be left alone to myself much like when I was a child. "Depletion" was the word he used. I would now be Number 2.

Of course I couldn't comprehend this concept back then. I maintained that I was fine and that I, in time, would become a totally different person on the day our daughter was born. Like magic, I would change.

The excitement about the baby wouldn't last. At week 28 we found ourselves in the hospital. Jen was lying in a bed with her feet elevated. She was put on bed rest and admitted to the hospital indefinitely. Then she was ordered to lie in that incline position for twenty-plus hours a day for the rest of the pregnancy. It was a difficult period for her and maybe even me, though I didn't know it. Jen was a labor and delivery nurse, so she knew more than me. She knew how serious this was. I had no clue.

So the next couple of months brought little change for me personally. The magical improvement wasn't evident. My days would be spent at work for a few hours, at the hospital with her for the afternoon, and home alone at night.

Alone at home, my demons rang often. Without anyone around, I spiraled. The days felt like weeks as the damage I was doing to myself compounded. I was sleeping a handful of hours every few days. I was exhausted, yet I couldn't show it. I still went to work and still showed up at the hospital. I was good at grinding through and faking it, but I remember vividly begging the sky for help.

As if bed rest wasn't enough, our little girl decided she'd had enough and wanted out. She was born prematurely at week 32. She fit in the palm of my hand, almost weightless. It was terrifying.

Her new home was not ours but the NICU for almost three weeks, with other children with similar challenges. We were with her every day but had to go home in the evening. Leaving her at night was tough. Eventually she showed signs of improvement. Because Jen was a trained NICU nurse, the hospital agreed to let us take her home.

We dove in as parents, and what I thought would happen was happening. I was off drugs and engaged. But, sadly, only until the "scare" period ended and a new normal set in. Jeckel had warned me: depletion.

I didn't know why and how Jen tolerated this tornado living in her home. I knew "'til death do us part" was not something she uttered just to go through the motions at our wedding. I knew she meant it, as did I. But this isn't what she signed up for, and I knew it. I tried hard to not think about our situation. I hoped it would just miraculously work out.

I never asked her why she stayed. I was afraid to know. So I made up my own "why" back then. I assumed it was a combination of the fact that she wasn't a quitter and that she knew that this isn't what I wanted for myself. This phase would pass. I believe she felt, like me, it would pass with age and greater responsibility. But, I didn't see the real "why" until much later.

Our challenging first pregnancy combined with the potential difficulty of getting pregnant a second time and the fact I wasn't in a great place took their toll. After considering having another child, we quit trying. The stress was crippling and the timing didn't seem right.

Months later, to our amazement and with complete surprise, we learned that Jen was pregnant. We were very excited and hopeful. But the hope and excitement was once again met with loving concern from Jeckel. "Depletion," he warned.

His warnings weren't helpful, though. Even if I did heed the warning, there wasn't really anything I could do about it. The snowball was getting bigger and bigger, and the bigger it got the smaller the possibility of stopping it. I was in less control of my life than I had ever felt. And at that point I was only a couple of years into therapy. While that may seem like a lot, it isn't really, for this type of therapy.

A few months into the pregnancy, my behavior was not improving. Actually, it was getting much worse. It got so bad that Jen asked me to move out. That's when I moved into the hotel.

Looking back, I'm proud of her. Jen's a strong woman. She did what she had to do for the sake of our children and her sanity. That took a lot of guts. She was pregnant and had a one-year-old, and she sent me a clear message. The message is clear today, but it wasn't then. Back then I was angry . . .

Only a couple of weeks into our separation, I got a call at work. She reluctantly asked me to come home. It wasn't that she thought I was rehabilitated; she was ordered to bed rest for the remainder of the pregnancy again. This time she needed me to take care of not only her but our first child, too.

I sprang into action. I will never forget this time. I minimized my responsibilities at work for the next few months and spent almost every moment at home that I possibly could. I bonded with my daughter. I fed her, bathed her, watched cartoons with her (I knew the words to all the cartoons' opening songs that we sang it together every morning), and played dress-up hours upon hours. I cooked, cleaned, and took as good care of my family as I was capable of—and I actually loved it! I was clean as a whistle.

This was one of the "why's" that kept Jen from giving up on me. Here was a side of me that didn't shine early in our marriage. I felt needed, and being nurturing felt natural. I was learning to understand love and even starting to recognize it. As I've described in earlier chapters, in many ways I operated better as a "fixer" of with challenges. This period gave me enough challenges and fixing to keep me occupied from morning until night.

Our second daughter was born on time and healthy. We quickly forgot about the crazy few months of confinement to bed because of the happy ending. I was relatively sober and back at work trying to grow my business. For the most part, the period between 2007 and 2010 was a very productive time for me. I worked my ass off, opened some more stores, and bought some more real estate.

The binges existed, but the frequency lessened. I had more physical responsibility and more pressure on my time. This affected the frequency, but when the opportunity arose, I still took full advantage. Knowing that my opportunities to completely "check out" and deaden myself were limited, the intensity of each instance increased. This off/on existence was my new normal.

I truly felt that the frequency of the binges was now under control. I'd brag to Jeckel, "I got this." I would even quote stats. "It's been twenty-six days, Doc."

His reaction was the same every time I spouted one of my self-anointed accolades. He would clench his lips and just smile, supportive but not in agreement.

I know Jen wasn't totally happy with me, but I think she was hopeful as she saw both glimpses of good behavior and my strong commitment to therapy.

When I told Jeckel we were having baby number three, he issued the same warning: "Depletion!" Only this time I would be bumped to Number 4. By now I was six or so years into therapy, and I was a believer in his wisdom. Before, I had blown off his warnings; this time I listened. (Jen, on the other hand, had figured this disruption out on her own. I know, because she hadn't told me she was pregnant again for months.)

I remember when she told me. She asked to have lunch together, and then very hesitantly spilled her concerns. She explained that she was worried about me going off the rails because I was in the middle of a very important acquisition in my business career. It was a strategic shift in my strategy of my company, and she knew it was a big moment for me in my career. The pressures at work and at home would be tremendous. She had clearly studied my pattern of behavior during our previous two pregnancies and she was apprehensive.

I was numb and silent as she spoke about the news. I was happy about the pregnancy and upset that she had withheld it for months.

I closed on my business deal, and I could hear the little voice in a corner of my ear . . . whispering ever so softly . . ."Depletion! Now you are Number 4!"

Fast-forward several months.

I traveled for work periodically, sometimes just a couple of hours away, but it wasn't unusual for me to do overnights.

It was on one of those overnights that I received a call. It was sometime around midnight. I looked at the caller ID and saw the three letters I didn't want to see: J-E-N. *Crap*, I thought. I reluctantly I answered the phone. (She was pregnant; I had to.) But I was off my rocker. I was in the middle of a dance with the devil and she was cutting in.

"I need you to come home now." She was having contractions. Our third daughter was on the way, and Jen knew it would take me a few hours to drive back so she wanted me to get on the road as soon as possible.

This was a problem. I remember looking to my right: a bottle of eighteen-year-old Macallan. I looked closer and saw that the bottle was about three-quarters empty. Or, if you wanted to be positive, you might say one-quarter full.

I then slowly turned my head to the left and looked at the

nightstand. I saw a little Baggie, white powder spilled every-where. It was on its last leg. I reached my hand to my chest, as I often did, to feel my pulse. My heart was pounding, somewhere in the range of 200 beats per minute.

I got off the phone, reassuring Jen that I would be on my way.

The good news was that I was only about three miles away from home, locked up in a local hotel. I wasn't visiting one of my stores. I had lied. I was so ashamed, literally in a panic trying to figure how to manage this.

I drank the remaining scotch in hopes of sobering up. Knowing Jen wouldn't be expecting me for a few hours yet, I set my alarm for 2:30 a.m. in hopes of getting a couple of hours of sleep.

The alarm went off, and I hadn't slept a wink. I had spent the last two hours just working on my breathing, downing mouthwash, scotch, and water. I took a shower, jumped into the car, and made that three-mile drive home.

I finally arrived at home around five in the morning, three hours later than she expected me. Jen was furious. We dropped off our six- and four-year-olds at a friend's house and drove to the hospital.

I had spent hours lying on the bed at the Comfort Inn thinking what it would it be like at the hospital. I was mentally preparing for disaster. I thought about the doctor asking if I was okay when I showed up in the state I was in. I would tell him my shaking was just excitement and nerves—*not* a bag full of cocaine in my body.

That was one of the worst experiences I have ever had, and

it could have been even worse on so many levels. It was one of my loudest wake-up calls. I remember thinking, *I never want to feel that away again.* Although this wasn't the end, it was the beginning of the end.

Remember the list of "why's" I shared at the beginning of the chapter? It was more than a commitment Jen made when we got married. It was a contract . . .

"'Til death do us part."

Why did my wife stick by my side? Why did my friends stick by me? How could they continue to love me when I, the very person they loved, was incapable of loving myself?

Jen sent me an email while I was writing this book. I had shared one of my chapters with her, one of the uglier ones.

She wrote: "I know the drugs had you, but I believe that the other side won the battle most of the time."

She chided me for being unsparing, unforgiving in presenting how my choices hurt me, my family, my friends, and my businesses. By doing so, she wrote, I minimized the joy and love I brought to the people I cared about. "Don't forget all the moments with friends that loved you for you."

Flooded with emotion, I tried to sort through this . . .

As disappointed as I was with myself, I couldn't comprehend the thing that I have searched for my whole life even though it was staring me right in the face. Right before me, I had a family that mirrored me so lovingly and without condition, the thing I had always wanted but missed through my distorted lenses.

I also had amazing friends who saw through my lies and

deceit yet maintained their love when (I thought) they should have quit on me. I never saw that or understood it.

The "why" is now so simple. Jen saw what I wasn't able to see—what Jeckel had told me all along. I already had the qualities that made me deserving of love.

The sweetness of this discovery is a blessing from the same sky that I often talked to as an adult and a kid. The credit is due to a culmination of years of therapy and dumb luck in finding the most amazing wife.

I believe in a commitment, and I believe in the power of loyalty. But, what my wife endured goes beyond that . . .

'Til death do us part!

CHAPTER 26

City of Blinding Lights

It was July 2011. Jen and I were in St. Louis with several couples for a weekend. The highlight of the weekend was a U2 concert at Bush Stadium. We had rented a skybox high up, overlooking the field, so high that Bono looked tiny on that stage.

There were maybe sixty thousand people in the stadium. I was blown away by the beauty and magnitude of the moment: the stage so grand, the music even more grand. I was captivated even more by the level of talent and accomplishment on that stage as well as the admiration from people in the crowd. What a spectacle.

A new song started and I heard a sequence of notes. I couldn't quite make out the instrument at first. Such a unique and beautiful sound. A guitar, but it wasn't obvious. That sequence played precisely four times. I drifted. This riff penetrated my body . . . then my mind.

I had never heard this song before, but it sang to me therapeutically. Sang to me emotionally. I have had this experience with music many times before, when a song strikes me so deep

I can feel it in my soul, raw and powerful. These reverberations are real feelings that sink in deeply and touch my soul.

When I have these feelings, I instinctively slip into analysis. I always think *why*? I believe with conviction that this analysis is the key to my development, the key to unlocking my true self. Generally, it's an emotion I have a hard time connecting to directly. Even in therapy I had a hard time articulating the feeling I was feeling as the U2 song drifted over the crowd and into our skybox and then my heart. The emotion was complex, many feelings all rolled into one. Sad, blessed, proud, and sentimental—all at the same time.

The song was called "City of Blinding Lights." I couldn't get it out of my head. It sent me deep into thought.

I was having a conversation with a friend, high up in that box, as I heard those notes for the first time. I continued my conversation all the while listening to the riff. Those notes just simply stuck.

I was deep in thought, and all the while I was having a conversation with my friend, my two selves having very different experiences at the concert. We were talking about drumming. I remember, in detail, the conversation with my friend. Yet I was in another world. Fully engaged in both.

I was thinking about what I was seeing. Bono was parading around on stage. He owned it. Jealous, I watched and wondered what it would be like to be in his body. I wondered what he was seeing. I imagined the exact image in front of him: a crowd of admiring fans. Dancing, smiling, and lip-synching along to the words he wrote.

I wondered if he was paying attention to what the fans were

doing? Did he see them air drumming? Did he see their arms
raised high up in the air, swinging away to the thumping of the
drum? Their faces full of joy! Friends and loved ones united,
moving in sync, with their arms wrapped around one another.

What was that like? I thought. I wanted to know so badly!

My thoughts then drifted farther. And in a weird way, I felt
sorry for him. I wondered: *What next? What happens after the
concert?* What happens after the lights go down and the cheer
of the crowd subsides? What do Bono and the rest of the band
do after the concert? Do they just get in a limo and head to the
hotel? Once there, what do they do? Order room service . . .
have some burgers and fries? Or just change, brush their teeth,
and go to sleep?

I realized I was sad for *me*. My observing ego pointed out
that I was projecting my own fears. This is easily one of my biggest fears: What happens after the fun ends? When the admiration ends? In the case of Bono, the fans innocently served as the
ultimate mirror. The type of mirror I've sought my whole life. I
couldn't imagine how the band must have felt. Right there, in
front of them, enough admiration to last a lifetime, if such a
thing exists.

I was nervous imagining what happened when Bono went
home. I wasn't well yet. My mirror was cracked. Less and less
cracked every day, but still cracked. My world was not integrated. *I* wasn't "integrated" yet. That's what Jeckel always said.
"You have to integrate." My multiple selves were not one, and
I still moved unconsciously back and forth through these different selves.

Had I been on that stage, I would have felt anxiety, knowing and fearing for the moment that I would have to exit stage left. I would have struggled, knowing this moment would end. From that high to nothing: a precipitous crash.

I would return to the hotel room without the image of myself that I saw reflected in the eyes of the crowd. I would be left alone with only my own reflection, an insecure little boy. To prevent the crash, I would have needed something to artificially keep it going. To be specific, I would have needed even more stimulus than the amount provided by those fans. Every high needed to be more than the previous high. Period! And after such a high, if I didn't plan accordingly, I would hear the calls from my demons. I would need my medicine.

Sadly, I wasn't yet the man I pledged to be. I wasn't doing my ritual and my drugs, but I knew then and there that I had a long way to go. Had Bono and I switched spots and it was me on that stage instead of him, I would not have gone straight to the hotel and to bed. Not me, not yet. I would have tattooed that city until the sun came up and consumed enough to make sure I either died or fell asleep. Anything to keep the high from crashing.

I told Jeckel about that whole experience. I couldn't get it out of my head. I must have listened to "City of Blinding Lights" a hundred times, over and over. I listened to that song on every drive to my sessions with Jeckel for the next several weeks. I was hoping that song could take me back to that feeling I had in the skybox. I wanted Jeckel and I to dig in. I wanted to know why that song affected me so much. I wanted to know why I would tear up a little bit every time I was alone and heard that song.

A month after the U2 concert, at five o'clock in the morning, I was listening to "City of Blinding Lights" as I was driving to a charity event that I had founded. That's when the little tearing up turned to a full-on cry. The tears flowed. I loved crying. Crying for me was a win. Every time I cried, I felt closer to myself. I felt closer to an "integrated" self.

This community event had long been a dream of mine. I badly wanted to do something that really impacted the community. I loved to raise money for local charities. Giving was in my nature. This was the first year of what would become an annual event.

I had enlisted a couple of my close friends to help me put on the event. We built this event from the ground up. No training or experience, just a will to do something meaningful. We built—from scratch!—a 5K obstacle course—and thousands attended! It was a huge success. Incredible!

Tears flowed as I pulled up to the site of the event. I was connected to my emotions at this moment. My dreams were actually aligning with reality. It was still dark, so I sat in my car, alone, and I cried. As I waited for daybreak, I asked myself, *Why are you crying?*

Was it because I pulled off an event that thousands of people would attend? Did I feel a great sense of accomplishment? Were they tears of joy? Maybe! Often in such moments I think about where I've been and where I am now. Didn't seem that long ago that I was a sad little boy admiring the carpet in the new grade school in California. It didn't seem that long ago that I was in Pakistan eating for the first time in days. It didn't seem that long ago I was riding that bus for a week, avoiding another new school in a town I hated—ironically, the same town I was now creating charity events for.

I sometimes can't believe it. It makes me feel . . . a unique blend of emotions. I think I would call it sad, blessed, proud, and sentimental—all at the same time. This was the exact feeling I had experienced in the skybox.

Another side of me, of course, wondered if the tears were from doing something that got me a *ton* of attention and admiration. If so, that was disappointing. But I'm trained to look at things from multiple sides and to always be aware of the side of me that is potentially a narcissist. I hate the word "narcissist" and I wish it gone. I will be complete and self-actualized when there is not a strand of narcissism in my body.

But narcissism is everywhere. It is something that will never perfectly be eliminated. As Jeckel explained to me, "We all have some narcissism in us." Things that we are deeply vested in—relationships or passion projects—are naturally somewhat narcissistic.

The question was, which narcissism was I feeling? I believe and hope it is the more innocent and less harmful one. The one that is a result of just being deeply vested in something. I see, and draw a fine line between, these two types of narcissism. When you are "vested" in something that you have worked hard for—in this case, this charity event— you can't help but find yourself feeling a bit of self-admiration. This, to me, is not unhealthy, especially if you are aware of it and understand it.

The narcissism that I hate is the one that you see in people who are extremely self-absorbed and selfish, coupled with a grandiose view of themselves—like I used to be. Maybe they put on a charity event, but only for the praise they get afterward.

I have had a hard time distinguishing which kind of narcissism is motivating me. When in doubt, I discuss what I am feeling with Jeckel. My goal is simple: to live a narcissism-free life. This would mean that I'm integrated and have found a way to distinguish myself from my true self and external things. I don't know if that day will come, but I make sure that every day is an improvement from the day prior. It's ingrained in me to think about it.

I think about this so much that I almost feel that therapy, especially psychoanalysis, is inherently narcissistic. After all, all you think about is yourself. "It's all about you." I feel guilty about this some days. I have brought this up in sessions, and it's hard for Jeckel to deny. My saving grace is that self-focus creates a healthier me, which makes me a better husband, father, friend, boss, and community leader.

That August morning as I sat looking forward to the silliness and fun of our 5K race to come, I hope that my desire to help the community and our local charities was real, integrated, and genuine. I hope that, at the very least, my narcissism was rooted in sincerity and charitableness.

I'm pretty sure it was, and that's why I cried.

CHAPTER 27

I Will Miss Robin . . .
Thank You, Jeckel

On August 11, 2014, I was out of town on business in Appleton, Wisconsin. I had dinner that evening at a Chinese place with my tire rep and my general manager. We had finished dinner, and I was patiently waiting for the prize. The waiter, right on cue, walked up to the table carrying a white plate with three little cookies wrapped in plastic resting in the middle of it.

It's a strange obsession, but I love fortune cookies. It's in my nature to be drawn to a hopeful future. The fortune cookie symbolizes that for me. I slowly unwrapped the plastic and gently broke apart the cookie (I almost never actually eat the cookie). Like a little kid, excited, I read the message to myself:

There are great things for you on the horizon.

It made perfect sense. *Fortune cookie makers know what the hell they are talking about,* I thought to myself. They clearly know how to get the right cookie with the right message to you. This was no mistake.

Joking aside, I was in a great place in my life. I was in

control and content. I was relieved to be so removed from the days where the devil and the power in that white powder in a little plastic bag had so much control over me. The relief I felt wasn't so much that I was clean, but that I knew that particular chapter was over forever. It was clear to me that my addiction issues were permanently over.

Sure, it was just a fortune cookie, but it was right. Good things were on the horizon for me.

I asked for another one. We were sitting at a table by the bar. I was chatting with some of the patrons and the bartender as well. I was bragging to them that my cookie was spot on. I went on to tell them that I was sure this next one would serve as proof that the first one was right. The two cookies would make sense together, thus proving my faith in the power of fortune cookies.

I did add a caveat: The next one had to be "perfect." In other words, the message of the two cookies had to fit together. The second fortune would have to match the meaning of the first. That'd be the only way for my fortunes to come true. I was confident.

Another cookie showed up minutes later. I was still excited, but now a bit more anxious and nervous. Like I was about to show off a difficult party trick.

You will hear kind words in the future.

It wasn't clicking. *Great things on the horizon . . . You will hear kind words . . .*

The fortunes didn't make "perfect" sense together. Now a bit embarrassed, I laughed it off and conceded that I couldn't win them all.

Then I got a text . . . from my wife. It couldn't have been more than a minute after my opening the second cookie.

I smiled.

"That's why all the more I'm proud of you!"

I jumped up and laughed out loud, a big smile on my face. People looked at me like I was crazy. It had happened! My wife's text was amazing. It would have made no sense to anyone but me. It meant a lot to me, and it made "perfect" sense. I had been right.

God bless whoever invented the fortune cookie.

I remember that date so vividly because, later that night, I heard the news: Robin Williams had died. The news coverage was insane. Initially, the details of his death were vague, and reporters were speculating about potential explanations. But I didn't need to speculate. I knew why this very special man had died . . . which made me even sadder.

Robin Williams was a legend, an American icon. I wasn't comparing myself to him. But I could relate. I could empathize with his sickness. I totally got it. Jeckel got it.

Hearing the news shook me up even though I didn't know this celebrity. I started having flashbacks. The memories took me back to some ugly days. Visualizing myself barricaded in a hotel room. Sick images forming in my mind. Images of a man caging himself, willingly, in this physical box of a room. The images were accompanied by strong emotions. The feelings of the same man caged in his mental box as well. It hurts my stomach just thinking about. It always does, and I suspect it always will.

The ugly images that I have actually lived and played out are still vivid.

The room is pitch dark, and I see the chair. The chair is pinned against the door. The TV is on mute. The window shades are aggressively manipulated and rigged so as to not show a speck of light. Bottles of booze on the counter, and me spread half-naked on the bed. I would try to make very few movements. Trying so hard to maintain complete silence. I just stare at the ceiling. My heart not cooperating, as usual. It's beating like a hammer. My body is trembling. And I'm scared. I'm a scared little boy.

Many of those nights I wanted to be done. It was getting old, and I was exhausted. Many of those nights I concluded, but only in my mind, that being done was the right thing to do. Just a few more lines and it could be over. Relief! During my binges, it was impossible to keep those thoughts out of my head. Man, things would be so much easier if I was just gone . . .

Lying on the bed, I would become filled with guilt. I was hurting so many people. I felt so much sadness. I was so disappointed knowing that I was a junky. I felt so much shame that this was actually happening to me. This only happens to other people, not someone smart like me. Not someone with so much promise. How did I get to this point? Yet here I was.

I don't know how it didn't happen. Not because of conscious intent, but because of an accidental overdose. At times so much poison flowed through me that I was sure my body would throw in the towel and just quit. White flags rose high and proud.

In those instances, when I thought my death was possible, I'd get dressed and quickly tidy up the area around me. I would think about how I wanted to be found. I imagined what people would think if they saw me a certain way. I wanted to be seen with a certain dignity. I didn't want to feel any more shame than I needed to. I didn't want to embarrass myself any more than I needed to.

I'd think of my loved ones—my family and my friends. I'd tell myself I could beat this. Just stay alive.

Then I'd start another routine. I'd focus on my breathing, and I'd check my pulse over and over and make sure I didn't fall asleep.

Back in Wisconsin, I woke up the next day a tad out of sorts and missing the hell out of my family. I had time to kill before I was to play golf in a charity event, and I needed a release. I decided to exercise. I hadn't brought shoes for this so I got into my car and drove to Wal-Mart. *Exercise will make me feel better,* I thought.

I put on some music, and shortly into the drive tears came to my eyes. It had been a few weeks. I needed to cry. For thirty-some years of my life I never cried; now, I crave it. I know the role it plays in my mental health. I love to cry.

I got the urge to call Jeckel.

"Hello," he said.

He said it again: "Hello?" And then one more time. I didn't

say a word. I just sat there with the phone in my hand. Silence. Then it came: no words, but the cries of a baby. I cried like a little baby. I don't know how long, but I never said a word. Jeckel just sat on the other end of the call and listened. Listened to me weep like a little baby. What seemed like minutes went by without a word from him or me.

Finally, he said: "Do you want to come in? I'll make time."

"I can't, I'm in Wisconsin," I said. "I just called to say thank you."

Then I hung up.

A lot of people think they know what it is. They think they know what depression is. Worse still, a lot of people think they understand it. Sadly, most people suffer from some form of depression. They just don't know they do—or they don't want to know it.

Most people think you have to be sad to be depressed. I never cried or felt sad in almost thirty years of my life, and I had severe depression. It comes in all forms and shapes. Some people just blast right through it, accomplishing and winning at everything that comes their way. Distracting themselves with short-term fixes: money, success, power, sex, booze, and drugs. Those are just a few of the usual suspects. Anything to ward off the feelings or connections to those feelings.

I'm not a clinical psychiatrist, but I have learned a thing or two, spending two or three times per week over the course of thirteen years with one. When I first learned (and eventually accepted) that I had depression, I decided to fix it. I fantasized about the day when it would be over. I thought that "someday" I'd be done. I had someday fantasies in many aspects of my life:

Someday I will be rich. Someday I will be respected. Someday I will have peace.

Those fantasies had one unrealistic vision tied to all of them: that when the someday comes, it will "perfect." The perfect part is common with people like me who have character sicknesses. My character defects, among many others, were narcissism, self-denial, an inability to mourn, and major swings in self-esteem. Effectively, my "self" was poorly integrated. (As I mentioned a time or two already, Jeckel and I spoke of integration with my true identity all the time.)

It was many years into therapy before I realized that there is no "someday" and "perfect" the way I defined them. I would have periods when my focus was laser-sharp in the pursuit of overcoming my addiction. I would be obsessed. Counting the days or months without the medicine. The longer I went, the closer I came to finding that someday: that perfection I was looking for.

I did this with great optimism until I had a setback. The smallest setback would regress me disproportionally. For me, it was basically intolerable to fail. It's the opposite of "perfect," that thing I prized so much. I would be so upset with myself when I failed. Jeckel always pointed out that I had unrealistic expectations for myself. These expectations weren't because I was a guy who just wanted to be great. It wasn't that I was someone who wanted to push himself to be the best he could. These expectations were part of my pathology. They were techniques to ward off deeper pains: pains of loss and wants not met. Nevertheless, for decades I pursued these desires unrealistically.

The ups and downs I experienced were a simple gyration

back and forth from a setback that would take the form of withdrawal. After a period of withdrawal, I would rebound with my auto-response. That response was to regain my optimism for the "someday." None of it was healthy, and this process was fruitless. It took a long, long time in analysis to start to unravel the strategies I had made for myself.

Depression is nasty and will grow with time if not dealt with. Everyone will have a different definition of what "dealing" with it means. For me, it was simple. Trust this doctor and follow the process. His process was simple as well: show up.

At times, when in a rut in therapy, I would get mad that I wasn't improving. I wanted more from Jeckel. I wanted answers and fixes. He'd reassure me that I just needed to show up. Many years later it became clear why I had to show up . . .

I had to be there when I was manic. I had to be there when I was grandiose and seemingly high on life. I had to be there when I didn't want to a say a word. I had to be there when I didn't want to be there. I had to go through all these vacillating periods of self-esteem and the conversations that came with them.

Not only was I learning a ton about myself, I was also building a strong connection with Jeckel. This connection and the work we were doing—slowly, but surely—provided some integration of my identities.

I thought of Robin Williams a bunch. I would imagine him getting ready to go onstage to receive some award in front of his peers—the best in the business. Thousands in the crowd admiring him and millions on TV doing the same.

I pretended to imagine what his hours leading up to that moment were like. Alone, maybe he felt the insecure Robin: the

Robin who decided to make millions laugh in order to shelter his deep sadness. The Robin who kept deep secrets about his core weaknesses. The Robin who saw his sadness grow increasingly more difficult to hide and deal with.

Over the course of this journey with Jeckel, I shed many tears. Most of those were from me getting in touch with some kind of childhood feeling. Sometimes this was intense, especially when I opened up complicated layers of feelings that I had suppressed.

For much of my life I focused hard on creating distractions from my sadness and disappointments. But when I did connect with my depression and the feelings within it, I benefited greatly. It's what brought me closer to my true self.

The tears I shed that August morning as I thanked Jeckel profoundly and then hung up were tears of joy. I was celebrating why I had to show up. I was building a real connection with an active listener I trusted—and a wise one at that. That connection was what gave me the strength to make that call. The simple fact that I could even pick up that phone was a monumental advance in my core strength. So vulnerable and so honest. But I did, and it felt good.

I felt the need to show my appreciation for his undeniable and unconditional love. As I said, I was in a good place. Things were coming together.

I knew I would remember that day forever.

I could have been Robin . . .

CHAPTER 28

Gaslight

One day in therapy Jeckel told me about a movie in which a husband manipulates his wife into thinking that she is going crazy. I had never seen or heard of this movie, but Jeckel began to tell me small pieces of the story in our sessions.

One of the main characters, a woman, is convinced by her husband she lost something that was given to her, even though she remembers clearly safely packing it away.

The husband later accuses the same woman of taking down a picture that she is sure she hadn't removed. Or had she? By the end of the conversation, the woman begins to believe him.

The woman notices a gaslight change from dim to bright. The husband suggests that the gaslight's fluctuation is a figment of her imagination. He manages to convince her that it's yet another one of her delusions.

I remember feeling sad the first time Jeckel described the premise of the story. I felt sorry for the woman in the movie. I couldn't possibly imagine being in the same position. The horror of someone purposefully constructing a false reality for me seemed so cruel.

The story also made me irately angry. I wanted to kick the shit out of the husband. I wanted to strangle him. I wanted to tell him that what he was doing was *not very nice*. I'd say, "Hey, asshole, that's not a fair way to treat someone." Then as I dwelt on it, I'd get even more upset and elevate my tone. "That's mental torture, asshole! How'd you like it if someone did that to you?" And then maybe I'd punch him right in the nose! I had this elaborate fantasy built around how I would punish this man who wasn't even real.

We didn't talk about this movie just once; it came up often. Every time Jeckel and I discussed the movie, something was triggered. The sense of empathy I felt toward the woman was strong. The hatred I felt for the husband was palpable. Suddenly, I would find myself sharing a story from my own life. It took me a long time to realize why I empathized with the wife and connected to her paranoia.

Over the years, I must have described to Jeckel stories and thoughts that made him want to tell me about this movie. He clearly saw a connection. He was smart to find an example, even if it was fictional, to access these emotions for me. He brought up the movie whenever my stories warranted a discussion about gaslighting, whenever I shared a feeling that held the same premise: a feeling of having your reality intentionally manipulated by someone else.

Arguably, gaslighting is borderline abuse. Jeckel really wanted me to understand this. He wanted me to internalize this concept, but he never pushed . . . as usual. Slow and steady we went.

At first I related to the gaslighting story only on an intellectual basis. I understood that there were similarities between some of my experiences with my family and the experiences this woman was having. I recognized that something about her story made me want to share more. That was as far as I got.

Interestingly, I focused more on her sadness than I did mine. I could connect that we shared a story, but her situation was the one that made me sad. It was her feelings I empathized with and felt. Her husband was the villain who enraged me. Clearly some tangled emotional thing had been touched in me, yet I couldn't connect it to my experiences in the same way, up until this point.

Relating to a concept intellectually is completely different from being able to internalize and emotionally comprehend the intended lesson. It's an entirely different experience to understand something than it is to *feel* it. It took me a long time to understand this concept. When you're emotionally in touch with something, you feel it. You feel it deep inside. If the message holds a painful truth for you, it hurts . . . it really hurts.

This clicked for me when I began recalling times in my life where I was gaslighted. Times when I would share my feelings or thoughts only to be met with how I was wrong. How I was wrong in my perceptions or how I was wrong to feel the way I did. The disconnect happened when my perceptions and thoughts didn't match the perception and thoughts that my parents had wanted me to have. If I didn't align with them, then I'd find myself thinking I was crazy. That was so damaging and enraging.

Fast-forward many years. More than a decade into therapy. And I tell Jeckel this story.

One Sunday in early March, my mom called to discuss our upcoming trip to visit her and my father for the Persian New Year, which is the first day of spring, March 21. New Year's Eve, March 20, is a big night in Persian tradition, like Christmas Eve for most Americans. You are supposed to gather with family, eat certain foods, and celebrate being together.

Mom asked—no, she begged—that I make no plans for the twentieth. (This trip wasn't just to visit them; it was also a vacation with our friends.) I assured her that we would absolutely make this night a priority and gladly keep March 20 open for them.

Three days later, she calls again. My mother asks what time she should make reservations for brunch on the twentieth.

"Brunch?" I ask. I don't remember a single conversation about brunch. In fact, I hate brunch. I've hated it all my life, and my parents know this. And here she is pushing brunch on me, something we had never talked about or I had agreed to.

As we are talking, a lightbulb goes off in my mind. It reminds me of the light from the gaslight. It's happening. Here comes the knot that usually forms in my stomach. I feel the tension deep in the pit of my stomach. I begin to feel hot. My face warms and my hands start shaking. The physical feeling is first, but I recognize I'm getting pissed, sad, and hateful all at the same time, even with all those years of therapy behind me.

I know why I'm getting sick to my stomach. I know my mom's tactics well, and it breaks my heart. My reaction is about more than just this one request, which seems so small but feels so big. Changing the plans is nothing I can't handle. I've seen it a million times. It's not the sudden change that hurts so much. It's her refusing to acknowledge that we had made one set of plans and then she made another without consulting me.

The sadness I feel is because she doesn't even realize that she is gaslighting me. It was easier to handle these situations when I was a kid. I didn't know any better. The emotions were there, but I never felt them. I was a human, but my feelings were protected in Bubble Wrap. Completely warded off and completely insulated.

But not today. Today, I feel it. And it hurts and sucks at the same time.

I regain my composure and decide to play it out. I remind Mom that she had asked that I keep this very important evening free to spend with the family to ring in the New Year. And I further remind her that she is now changing our plans and asking for a brunch.

"What has changed?" I ask.

"Oh, nothing," she says casually. "One of our friends invited us to dinner that night, and oh yeah, they invited you guys as well. They'd love to have you guys come with us . . . they love you guys so much and want to see you as well." She catches herself and quickly adds, "I told them that you guys would probably not want to come, though, since you had friends in town."

At least that last statement was true.

I say okay and hung up. I was standing in my kitchen when

I got off the phone. I sat down, took a deep breath, and laughed out loud.

For once in my life I thought and wished she could just speak to me, acknowledging that I am a human with a memory. Did she just assume I forgot what a big deal she made about keeping that evening free because it's an evening that should be spent with family? Does she think I'm stupid and that I don't get that, when offered the chance, she would rather go to her friends, instead? Does she really think it would bother me if she just told me the truth—that they want to be with their friends?

She could have just said they would love to be with their close friends and that they would also love to spend time with us and wanted to try to manage all of it. I would have been so happy to hear the truth. The problem is, in her world, she does it unconsciously.

Narcissism is a crazy lens through which to see the world. If you are a narcissist, you have no idea, by definition.

How many times had I heard, "No, no, honey, that's not what we said . . . You must have forgotten . . ."

My parents don't know they are doing it. They just can't help themselves. God bless them; as I've said in earlier chapters, they mean no harm or malice. It's just how they are programmed. It's all happening unconsciously. They'll never get it. Never.

When I set out to write this book, I feared a few things. Hurting my parents' feelings was at the top of the list. But, the reverse of that fear was also true. I was terrified that this book would dredge up old memories of how much they had hurt me. And that also meant that everything—from the events, to the thoughts, to the feelings—would be brought up and dissected.

Every story would be contested by my mom and dad. Every feeling I had or have would be discounted and met with their doubt and skepticism. And, as usual, with no sympathy.

The good news is that I have made a conscious and productive effort to not let the criticism affect me. My well-being is now at the forefront. I've reached a place where their reaction means less to me.

It's hard enough as a grown man in his forties to operate with these strange dynamics, as you can see from the story I've just told. I can't imagine what it must have been like being a victim of gaslighting as a child, without the luxury of twelve years of therapy to help deconstruct what was really going on.

When I look back upon my life, it's always with a sense of shame; I've always been the one to blame . . .

I'm reminded of a line from a Pet Shop Boys song that speaks of a person who feels ashamed of his life and takes the blame for everything that happened in it. I relate to that line because I've always felt like it was about me. Children almost always blame themselves for everything that happens in their lives. When parents fight, they think it's because of them. When parents divorce, kids blame themselves. When parents don't show their love or empathy, their kids wonder what they did to cause this.

I was no different. *I've always been the one to blame* is an underlying current that lives in my body today. But it lives differently in my body today then it did many years ago. No matter how carefully I craft this story around the parts that involve my family, I will lose. No matter how thoughtfully I present the picture of my world, I will still be the "crazy one." In their mind, I'm to blame.

It's always me that's "off" if my thoughts deviate from the world in which my parents live. They see things entirely differently. Whether or not I choose to accept their reality, I still have to live with some of the consequences. I have now accepted this.

I know we all have things that our parents do or say that drive us batty. The question is why? Many people I know just say, "Oh well, that's just how my parents are!" I was one of those guys. I accepted it and didn't for a second think about why. The consequences, for me, of dismissing how my past informed my present were pretty severe. So dismissing it wasn't an option if I wanted to be healthier person.

I'm not suggesting that you should dwell on your past for the rest of your life. But I am suggesting that you shouldn't just "get over it," either. I think it's important to analyze how you've become who you are, especially how your parents have shaped that journey. How your childhood journeys have shaped you. Not so you can dwell endlessly on injustices and continue to live in the past. Not to continually relive your anger and hurt and further enrage yourself. And, most importantly, not to hold grudges for the rest of your life. That would be foolish and unfair to the people around you. Studying our past is no different from studying history. We do it to learn and better ourselves.

I needed the analysis to understand the concept of gaslighting and how it related to my childhood injuries. It is a fundamental piece in my pursuit of integration.

CHAPTER 29

Perfect Pain, Part I

I honestly don't know why I started writing this book. It just happened one night. I suppose that writing is, in some ways, therapeutic for me. I tend to talk to myself a lot—not out loud, but in my own mind—as a comfort. I was my own best friend for a long time. Maybe writing is an evolved form of talking to myself.

I've been talking to myself for as long as I can remember. I was anything but one person. Yes, I had one physical body, but inside my body lived multiple people that didn't share the same mindset at all times. These alternative minds were simply sharing a body. They were nothing alike. In fact, and unfortunately, my mind closely resembled two roommates who were put together against their will.

My conflicted personas talked to each every day for decades. Back and forth they went. Sometimes they spoke to one another with respect. They would even listen to one another's thoughts. Half the time they even respected one another's differences of opinion. However, the other 50 percent of the time, it was all-out war. This led to a total disconnect within me, the opposite of integration. Sometimes it took months before they made up or spoke to one another.

It was about five years ago when it just kind of happened. One night, overcome by emotion, I started writing this book in my head. I was feeling rough and raw at this point in my life—unafraid to be real or painfully honest with myself. I felt this need to put a pen to paper.

I was reflecting about my crazy rituals: that insane place I created both in my mind and in the bathroom. I was reflecting on how many hours I spent locked up in this dungeon that had felt so safe. Looking back, I couldn't believe I did this for a decade and somehow survived it.

I had this need to come clean. To tell my story. I lived with a secret that so few knew about, and I hated that. I felt I couldn't move forward if I didn't do this. I hated the fact that so many people respected me without knowing the whole story. I felt it wasn't genuine. I felt like people that I cared about were partially bamboozled and that didn't sit well with me.

At my core I have always believed there was a deeper purpose to life, perhaps more than we know or are capable of comprehending. My actions didn't always support that view. But, ever since high school, I have always felt, deep down, that life is more than houses, vacations, popularity, and all the other superficial bull crap. I knew this because, at my lowest moments, I always pondered the big picture.

Alone, privately, I connected to a world that was thousands of miles away. A world in which children are exposed to things that no human should be exposed to. A world of war, death, and suffering. A world so unfair and cruel on levels that I have never had to endure and at levels I've never felt. I remember life in Iran enough to be able to connect to a world that is so incredibly different from the world I live in now in the United States.

Life now is so different from in the Middle East. I have always felt guilty about living in America while the rest of my family still lives in a country where analyzing their emotional needs would seem so silly and ridiculous. Most of my family in Iran is struggling to procure the basics of survival. Many are having to deal with the loss of loved ones. When I look around the world, my issues seem small. Nonetheless, I was where I was and was clearly sick. If I hadn't fixed my problems, I would have inflicted tremendous pain on my loved ones.

Early on in my struggle, I resolved this conflict with the guilt I felt using the discoveries of a physicist. I used Albert Einstein's theory of relativity, or at least a simplified version. His explanation was complicated and mathematical, while mine was simple. Maybe he was talking about physics, but life and experiences are relative as well. What is significant to a child in the Middle East could be quite different from what an American child thinks about.

I didn't know what I didn't know. It was only until I saw a contrast that I realized there was a difference. For example, kids in the Middle East are so exposed to war and conflict that they essentially know no different. It's their normal. It's only when you see another vantage point that you realize the craziness of the world you live in. Had I never left Iran, I wouldn't be writing this book and talking about my childhood needs that went neglected. I would have been reflecting about something entirely different, perhaps needs on a more basic and primitive level.

Life, to me, no matter the zip code, is about connecting to the "human" inside us. In my opinion, to be in touch with your humanity requires a deep level of honesty with yourself. I believe it's a foundational piece of our humanity, the common thread between us, no matter what continent we live on.

I am convinced that you can never be *unhappy* if you are true to yourself. Being true to yourself means that, good or bad, you are in touch with what's going on inside you. In my opinion, it's the most powerful thing anyone can accomplish. Identifying with your *true self* and finding your most authentic self is perhaps one of the secrets to life. Once you find this authentic self, hopefully, you still like yourself. That's the crème de la crème.

I've had a relentless, maybe even obsessive, pursuit of this truth ever since I can remember. Even in the days when I was stretched naked on the bed of a hotel room on the brink of never turning back. Or sitting alone, locked in a bathroom. Those days when I was basically pouring gasoline on the fire that was my existence and knowingly putting a match to it. Watching myself burn but doing nothing about it as the fire raged out of control.

There was a silhouette of me, slowly burning and smoking, watching my life turn to ashes right before my eyes. Even then, that twisted, destructive "me" was searching for something bigger and more meaningful.

Since I can remember, the bigger my mind thought, the more I was convinced this physical world we live in was a joke.

I don't mean that in a dismissive or disrespectful way. I don't mean that life and this world weren't something to cherish or take seriously. In fact, quite the contrary.

This thought process helped me try not to take things too seriously. Initially, this way of thinking served as a form of denial. If I don't take anything seriously, then I don't have anything to lose. The world was too much for me in many ways. There were too many inconsistencies and too much unfairness for me to be able to accept it as real. So I thought of it as joke.

I plowed ahead with my delusions. Greatly misguided in my priorities, I succumbed to life's rich demands. I was sick. With a multitude of excuses, I allowed my narcissism to pave the road ahead and guide my decisions. That radically colored my perception of the world.

I passionately pursued all the things our society admired: power, money, and popularity. I was very conflicted. As I pursued all the bull crap, I knew my motives were not healthy. However conflicted and aware I was, I still did it.

Looking back, I know why I did. Unconsciously, I did it just to do the all the things that I thought society rewarded. I pushed hard so I would never have to do it again. And once that was done, I could get on with working on living as a "human." I could then pursue the big-picture needs and the wants that my soul required. I wanted to cherish the things that really mattered, without any regret. I wanted the love of "human" connection. That's what matters most to me.

The dark times in my recent past had a similar feel to my days with my cousin. I did what I had to do with my cousin just to get it over with. The end justified the means. Whoring myself to the world was no different. It was the means to the end. The end is what I wanted. The end, I hoped, would justify the means.

I have hurt a lot of people over the last decade. Mainly my wife, my kids, and my close friends. My close friends—they know who they are—have loved me through some shitty times. I was an exhausting narcissist. I owe them so much for sticking with me. And then there are my wife and kids, my true heroes. What they did was something that I had never experienced. They simply loved me unconditionally.

Brian, one of my best friends, asked: "Why? Why do you want to expose all this? This book will make it hard on your family. It could embarrass or hurt them."

"*Exactly,*" I told him . . .

I am not excited about exposing my children to parts of this book that will make it any harder on them than it has already been. I surely don't want to embarrass them. But they are the reason I wrote this book. I feel that this will not only help shape my heart but it will also help shape their hearts.

I have three daughters. I love them more than anything in this world. They look at me like a rock star. They adore me as much as I adore them. They think I'm *perfect!* We all want and wish to believe our parents are *perfect*. And sadly, most of our parents really rely on this "need" to be held in that light. But that's bull crap and unfair. No one is *perfect*.

Kids adore their parents, and that's all well and dandy. But, wouldn't we all benefit from the truth? Why live in an unrealistic fantasy world regarding our parents? This unrealistic fantasy is what crippled me for most of my life. For me, it would have been wonderful knowing that my parents weren't *perfect* and, more importantly, that they were content with this truth about themselves. I would have loved them the same.

So why did I write this book? Why would I want a twelve-year-old, a ten-year-old, and a six-year-old to read or know that their dad was a drug addict? Why would I want them to know what a terrible father I was when they were young? Why would I want them to know what I put their mother through for so many years?

I unconsciously took advantage of the fact that they were little, trusting kids without a say in my choices, and that no matter what I did, they would love and respect me because I helped birth them. Why wouldn't I need to earn their respect and love? Should I expect them to adore me because they have to and because those are the rules?

Hogwash! I was the worst father a child could have, while they were just little, trusting kids, and they need to know that.

I want them to know all of this because it's the truth.

I have lived an entire lifetime searching for *perfect* in a world where *perfect* doesn't exist. And yet I kept trying to push that round peg into a square hole for such a long time. This gave me nothing but poison in my veins. This crazy pursuit of *perfect* was distorted. I was looking at the world with the eyeglass in reverse.

From a psychoanalytic point of view, this pursuit of *perfect* was explainable. When you are a little boy—a little boy who felt damaged and *imperfect*—you search for ways to soothe yourself with the fantasy of *perfection*. I lived with the hope that *perfect* was just around the corner. Someday, it will all be *perfect*. Somehow, someway, it will be *perfect*.

This was my fix for overcompensating for the real feelings I had of being insecure, unprepared, and ashamed. I just wanted to make momma so proud. Like a baby crying out for attention.

I don't want to protect my kids from the world. I prefer to prepare them for the world. I'm certain that they will be well-integrated children and later well-integrated adults, knowing that their parents, or dad in this case, was comfortable with the truths of life. They will be better off for having a dad who could admit his faults, inconsistencies, and insecurities.

If we don't do this, we then risk our kids feeling they can't accept all the parts of themselves, either. This, in turn, creates the possibility that our children might pursue the same remedies I did in order to not only protect themselves but also satisfy their parents' insatiable and false sense of themselves. It's a strange thing to wish, but I want my kids to know that they can be insecure, afraid, and disappointed. I know firsthand what happens when, as parents, we don't make this possible.

I believe the truth trumps everything. My children deserve the truth. And now, I'm not afraid for them to see my weaknesses. Having them know about my decade of sin will not only improve our connection but also, importantly, allow them to feel "free" to be themselves without judgment or fear.

"*Your dad is far from perfect, so don't feel you need to be.*"

That's my message to them.

Protecting my kids from the realities of life is the opposite of the way I was raised. I was *decided for*. It was decided that I couldn't handle the truth.

Dear Mom and Dad,

"Life ain't that big of a deal" . . . chill, and quit being so afraid, and stop taking it so seriously.

I would have much preferred the hard truth when we left Iran. I would have much preferred the hard truth that our life was about to really change.

Mom, I was raped repeatedly by your nephew, my cousin, and look at me . . . I can handle more than you think.

What I can't handle are your well-intentioned lies and continual need to be PERFECT. You're not perfect, and I love you the same. What makes me sad is having to reconcile the people you wish me to believe you are with what I see and experience. I would have nothing but admiration if you just talked to me with an authentic voice.

Life happens, and some people get handed some really bad stuff. Most will navigate those hardships with strong parenting and love. And to me, strong parents means "honest" parents: parents capable of handling imperfection. Capable of accepting imperfection in their child, themselves, and life circumstances. If they don't, then we internalize imperfections as fault, a recipe I don't recommend.

As a kid, I used to stare at the couch in our living room. A clear plastic cover stretched over it. This practice wasn't unique to my household. Many Persians do this, covering their couches so as to not inflict any wear and tear on these *precious* items. *Bull crap,* I used to think.

I remember when my kids were little, playing with their toys and abusing them, how much it used to bother me at times. I cringed when I saw the toys being rammed against one another and completely disrespected. How dare they actually play with their toys that way!

Then, in a defiant moment, I would join them in destruction. *I* would take their toys and ram them into the wall or other toys to express my distaste for my initial impulse, the one that I was taught that valued having no blemishes on our worldly possessions. Overvaluing stuff was symptomatic of this sick worldview I'd been raised with.

In my opinion, love is everything. This is what life is all about.

How can you love if you're not in touch with the truth of who you are? They go hand in hand. Love acts in the "present." It's not analyzing what to say or how to be. It just loves in the moment and it leaves everything out there.

So here I am, leaving everything out there . . .

I want to wash away the dirt of a decade of sin and let mercy come. I want to let go of what I've done and the pains I've caused and begin forgiving myself.

This is why I would give a book full of drugs, rape, and depression to my young and impressionable kids. I love them, but even more importantly, I trust them with this information. I trust it will only provide them with more strength.

They are little people with their own thoughts that I don't want to manipulate but only support. I'm not their boss. I intend to give them what wisdom I have accumulated over time, but I will never tell them how to be their authentic self. They are not *perfect* and neither am I. How awesome is that? They will make mistakes, and I'll love them just the same.

I will love them unconditionally and be proud of every thought that exists in their minds. Of course, like most parents, I hold my breath and worry if they may go off-script and think or do something I don't recommend. But I think it's a tremendous feat if you can just trust them—like I wished I was trusted.

Being able to love our children authentically is what gives them some of their core strength. I want my children to be strong. This is what most parents ultimately want for their children, but most of us, as parents, are poorly equipped to provide this. We protect and fix in the name of love, with good intention. We think it's the right thing to do.

In some instances it is, but only if we do it with the underlying notion that our kids are a unique brand and deserve to explore themselves. It may not match the thoughts or ideas they have that we would choose for them, but, as parents, we must respect that. I must allow my children to form their own identities, imperfections included.

A true sense of our own self is critical. Otherwise, we navigate with faulty radar on this great journey and tragically pull our children along for the ride. The point of our journey is to never arrive.

If we are in the present, we can go through life with the curiosity of a child. Wandering this earth on a highway that is not clearly marked. Not looking back and not anxiously looking forward. Just moving a day, an hour, or a minute at a time.

Never making light of life, but never taking it too seriously either. It's too short and unpredictable to think we can master it.

If I must master something, then I choose to master my relationships with humans.

I often, since I can remember, have wondered why we are here on this earth.

I don't know, but I do know it's not to be *perfect.* I also know it's not to live for this "someday" in the future that doesn't exist. It's to live for now. To love and hold tightly to your loved ones and to find and live out the most authentic and real version of yourself.

I still use the word "perfect" way too much. My parents use it even more. It's a word that I wish to eliminate from my vocabulary. I continually remind myself not to use it. I'm not there yet. And I am sure I will never get there, but I find great joy in pursuing improvement on a daily basis.

There is a purpose for me out there somewhere, and if I don't keep pushing myself and thinking about it, it will not be found. Finding a meaning and purpose for my life is a process that I enjoy deeply.

As I sit here today, I have learned so much in the last decade. I have learned to avoid being judgmental or critical of the events, people, and circumstances that life presents me. I work exhaustively to not assign "good" or "bad" to events and circumstances that come into my life. I try very hard to look at an event as just an event. I don't have a crystal ball, and I would be misguided if I thought I knew whether an event was or wasn't good.

A good example is this book. My old self would have placed

great importance on the success or failure of this book. Of course I want this book to be read by lots and lots of people. Of course I dream about it maybe inspiring someone. But that's not something I can control or have a desire to dwell on.

When I set out to write this, I had one goal: to finish it. Whether it's a *New York Times* bestseller or a book that only my friends and family read, my goal will have been accomplished. It is what it is.

I have a thought that has traveled with me across many decades. I think about the cells in my finger. Millions of them bouncing around and having a party in a one-square-inch area in the tip of my finger. Each doing its job. Each performing a very important function in my existence. Yet none of those cells know my name. None of them even know one another. They don't even know what a finger is, nor do they know the role they play in helping me type this paragraph.

I imagine my existence similarly to those cells. I haven't made sense of this world or our purpose here. I just know there is no way we don't have purpose. I have to imagine that this physical world is just mere passage into something more meaningful.

Even if I'm wrong, that thought gives me the peace I need to relax and live in the moment as much as I can. It's not easy. I am a work in progress.

My new *perfect* is to slow down and "sit" in the moment. Jeckel often encouraged me to sit in my depression. Sit in my pain. Embrace it and try real hard to not run or distract myself out of it.

It was when I learned to *not* medicate myself when I was

struggling that my struggles became not struggles but just life. The longer I could stay with it and the longer I could avoid running from it was the precise moment I knew my life would always be perfect.

Good or bad, that's perfection.

CHAPTER 30

Perfect Pain, Part II

Regrets, wishes, and what-if's . . . these are words and concepts that I would like to permanently erase from my mind and vocabulary. I'm not at that place yet.

But I am certain about one thing: I wouldn't change a single thing about my life. I don't wish for a single thing to be different. There is no event, person, or experience I wish erased. Sure, I have many regrets, like the harm I inflicted on myself and my loved ones for over a decade. I have wishes that went unfulfilled. But, I would never—truly never—want to go back in time and change a thing.

Not a single thing.

There is an old adage that says we can't know where we are going without knowing where we have been. In other words, it's important to understand your past as a guide in your journey.

Studying the past will provide learning and wisdom that can help eliminate future mistakes. Other times, the past can serve as a window into the future, a glimpse into who you're becoming and where you may be headed. This principle is what makes history so important.

What interests me even more is the history of my psyche: the *how* and the *why* I am *who* I am and *whom* I'm becoming. I would make one small change to that old adage. It's true that we can't know where we are going without knowing where we have been, but I also feel we can't know *who* we are without knowing *why* we are.

I've spent hours in that little room with Jeckel studying *why* I am the way I am. Over twelve hundred hours.

Initially, most of those hours were spent learning the basics. The first hundred hours or so were spent learning the alphabet, the "ABC's," the basics of the process by which psychoanalysis lives and operates. I also had to learn the basics of my own personal operating system.

I know now that from the beginning Jeckel knew exactly where I needed to go. He knew I had to get to the source of my shame, insecurities, and hurt that caused the pain I felt inside. But, masterfully, he allowed me to steer the ship. He could have easily manipulated the sessions in order to get me to think about what he felt I needed to be thinking about and working on. So much time could have been saved.

But that's not the process. I had to be ready. When a student is ready, a teacher shows up. A teacher may appear right in front of you, but only when a student is ready can you recognize the teacher. I had to know the multiplication table before I could multiply—and Jeckel doing my math for me wasn't the same as me doing it for myself.

The process in due time, with clear intent and willingness

from me, would organically delve deeper and explore the feelings and experiences I needed to explore. Feelings I never knew existed. Events I completely blocked out. How deep we went was a function of the amount I could simultaneously *tolerate* and *comprehend.*

Therapy was a ride. So many nuances. Once in a while, out of nowhere, something amazing would happen, sitting in the chair or lying on the couch. I would get in touch with something foreign to me, past feelings I never knew existed. Consumed with pain, my tears would flow. I'd cry like a baby. These cries were from depths I never imagined or knew existed. We don't know what we don't know.

Over time I got better at connecting with past emotions. Over time I got more and more comfortable with crying. Over time I became comfortable crying in front of another person, even a man.

Other times, something different would happen, something very different from tears. I would get in touch with my anger and rage. The kind of rage that explained all the fights I used to get in. The kind of rage that explained my temper that could be triggered by seemingly minor events. At times, Jeckel would see the rage acted out right there in that little office. He observed my childlike temper tantrums of monumental proportions, but he just calmly served as my punching bag.

He was my mirror. He provided me the kind of mirror I needed so badly. Never an ounce of judgment. He just listened and felt everything I was feeling with me. He rode my emotional roller coaster with me, over and over. The tantrums were childhood anger that I never got to experience, feelings that came to the surface decades later. Childhood anger that was previously forbidden, suppressed for decades.

Psychoanalysis sent me on emotional journeys that had me so puzzled and also so intrigued. Crying one day, angry the next, and completely paranoid the day after. Being emotionally flooded on a daily basis was the new norm. But working through these vacillating emotions was where the magic lay. I just had to keep showing up. And I did.

Bottom line: Over time I slowly developed the ability to feel these emotions that I hadn't felt before. I was dredging up and living in the present the feelings that had been buried and locked away for decades.

At first, it felt like these feelings were coming out of nowhere. It was like they just appeared, often without a trigger or any relevant events in my current life to connect them to. I always thought you needed to connect your current emotional state to something that was going on in your current life.

If I was frustrated, I wanted to connect and blame my emotion on something that was happening now, whether getting cut off on the highway or a bad day at work. I never thought my emotions might be connected to something deeper, something farther in my past.

Over time I realized that my feelings and emotions were grounded in something much deeper than the present moment and separated by space and time. I had an undercurrent of issues that were always there, although not always easily accessed. But they were there and it affected my psyche and decisions every minute of the day.

In that little room I learned the psychological equivalent

of the notion that correlation does not mean causation. Connecting the dots was not as simple and obvious as one might think. In fact, I discovered that for most of my life, my internal analysis of situations was generally inaccurate. I had so many outdated, irrelevant, and flat-out wrong reaction formations to events, my thoughts, and circumstances. Bottom line: I was wrong a lot.

For example, one of the things we talked about is the anxiety and fear I have of being poor. This fear was complicated, but it's about control and shame. Having money meant control. To me, having control meant having "no lack of control" (it sounds obvious, but this is an important distinction). A lack of control was something that I had felt for a great deal of my childhood. I felt like a yo-yo that moved up and down, but I never knew if I was on the way up or the way down. I hated that feeling, and, over time, the *hatred* of that feeling became burned in the fat cells of my brain.

Then one day, out of nowhere, I'd play out these fears. I'd all of a sudden slip into a state of paranoia, a panic attack, so to speak. I'd get so worried about money. These attacks weren't temporary. They lasted weeks and months. Most times these states were not founded in today's reality. There was no logic to it. It didn't apply to anything currently happening in my life. These attacks would appear without any reason to think that being broke was even possible.

The other side of the fear of being poor was related to shame. I felt that having money would somehow eliminate the feelings I had as a kid in America with an accent and a name that wasn't normal. With money, I thought I would be respected. Perhaps, somehow, people would overlook the fact that I looked different from them.

Another prime example was my reactions to having kids. In all three instances I completely lost my mind. It was the same issue I had with being broke. But I wasn't worried about financial depletion; this time the currency was love. With each kid there would be less love to go around from my wife. The kids would "steal" that, and I internalized it.

I would now be less relevant than I was before as each kid entered the equation. I would now be "love" broke. The love I needed from Jen would shift to the kids. Unknowingly, this set me off every time Jen was pregnant. But, I only really understood it by the time I had my third child. I actually know with certainty that my dad felt the same way.

No one knew I had all these fears. No one knew the states of panic I shifted in and out of. I never showed it, and I hid it well. These underlying fears would create so much anxiety and paranoia in my mind. Fear controlled and hijacked my mind on a daily basis. I spent so much time fearing that everything would fall apart and that I would be broke, both financially and emotionally.

Then Jeckel would remind me that I'm "*off.*" He'd point out the facts, compiling evidence that this sort of reaction was not warranted. At first his logic didn't help. I'd disregard what he said and allow the anxiety, fear, and reaction formations to control me and make me feel like shit. I think it's already been established that I had a distorted view of myself, but this was a particularly vicious habit.

Another way to describe this very "*off*" perspective is similar to the way people with an eating disorder see themselves.

They may stand on a scale, look down, and see eighty-five pounds—yet think they are overweight. Sadly, I can relate to that. Whatever the numbers read in my bank account, all I saw was bankrupt or broke. This negatively affected my already fragile and inconsistent self-esteem.

As a result, my image of myself and my world changed daily because of my poorly regulated self-esteem system. I swung back and forth, but eventually I'd come out of this state much like I did coming out of a three-day binge or an acid trip. In both cases, I found myself riddled with wonder at how I could ever have gotten so "*off*" and been so incorrect in my assessments.

Eventually, with a lot of work, I realized that I was simply playing out certain childhood fears, decades later. My fears sprang up without warning and for no apparent reason. These episodes followed no particular cadence and had no sense of timing. These states had zero links to the Parham of today and to my present challenges and life.

Unfortunately, though, these mental intruders played a strong role in my pathology and my misguided analysis of the world. Over time, I realized this and learned to manage the destructive nature of these intruders.

This is precisely the reason we need to know where we have been and *why* we are.

These examples may seem like common sense and something easily reconciled, but simply having awareness of the "why" I was having these attacks wasn't the fix. It was, of course, an important and essential start.

I clearly understood the link between my desires and the "why" of my desire for them. Take success (power), for example.

Success was a huge part of my wishes and needs. It had become the medicine that temporarily numbed my feelings of shame and helplessness. Success meant power. Power meant respect. Respect meant I no longer felt ashamed. I no longer felt like that Iranian kid with a terrible accent in an all-white school.

So, while I was gaining intellectual understanding of *where* my desires came from, my intellectual understanding was only the start of the fix. The second part of the fix was for me to actually *feel* that shame. I needed to *feel* exactly how I felt walking through that hallway in fourth grade in California for the first time. A week or so prior, I had been in Iran, playing soccer with Iranian kids in an Iranian school speaking a completely different language. I needed to *feel* how nervous I was to speak. So scared to pronounce an English word incorrectly.

I needed to *feel* the shame I felt for having different color skin from most of those kids and a funny accent. I needed to *feel* the shame I felt knowing that I was an Iranian immigrant that fled here to escape persecution while everyone was talking about how bad Iranians were because they were holding hundreds of Americans hostage at the time.

Finally, I needed to *feel* how angry I felt as a nine-year-old thrown into this new country with zero notice and zero understanding as to what the hell was going on!

So much I needed to feel . . . so much I needed to reconcile.

I also needed to *feel* what my nine-year-old self felt when my cousin, who I thought was my best friend, betrayed me. I needed to *feel* how hurt my feelings were when I realized that he didn't love me. If he really loved me, he would have never done what he did.

It was like falling off a cliff. The shock I felt when he first forced me into that mechanical room wasn't painful because of the actions that followed. The pain came from knowing that everything you knew and felt about family just imploded. I had a crisis of faith, but my "faith" had been family and love. My feelings were so hurt. He hurt my feelings more than anything you can imagine.

I needed to *feel* all of this to move on.

The fix to my emotional trauma was so much more than just remembering it. Of course, I had to remember before I could *feel*, but then I had to learn how those events played a role in how I got to where I got.

Why did the pain manifest itself in the form of me locking myself in a bathroom for hours on end? How'd I somehow build a successful company and how'd I somehow marry an amazing woman? What made me want and desire to be my high school's homecoming king so badly? And how had I actually accomplished this?

Why am I so sure that simply being aware cannot be the fix?

I had slowly become in touch with my desires, and, in most cases, achieved many of them. I had achieved as many of those childhood desires and wishes as I could. And the more of them I achieved, the worse my insecurities got. The worse my depression got.

The reason I got worse, simply stated, is that I was doing all of this for the wrong reasons. I wasn't solving my real issues. I was simply warding them off. To really "fix" my issues, I had to reconstruct and rebuild the foundation from the ground up. I had to get strong in order to create solutions that could be lasting.

We can all think of examples of hundreds of famous people who achieved the most impossible things, who went from nothing to something. You look at their lives, where they've been, and what they had to overcome. We admire these people. We love those stories. Why?

They overcame so much to get what they have: money, notoriety, acclaim.

Generally, though, people who are so obsessively driven to find that kind of mega-success have deeper issues haunting them. Their inspiration is some form of hurt or pain. They do and did everything they could to ward off those painful feelings with superficial "fixes," creating distractions to avoid and push away any undesirable pain.

I know this because I did it. I unconsciously tried to fix and right all the wrongs with success. The lucky ones of us, the properly integrated achievers, escape the illness. But most don't. Most aren't close to being anywhere near integrated. Those who aren't predictably implode and self-destruct. You see this every day. We find it so curious and interesting to watch. It's why we love reality shows. We see athletes and actors with the world seemingly in their hands and yet, predictably, we watch them fall apart.

Many of these amazing people take their unique talents to amazing heights in order to overcome their unmet needs from way, way back. It's their form of compensation. I observe and validate this notion every time I learn that an actor or a famous artist killed him- or herself. When I see this, I sadly think, *Yup* . . . and I get it.

Oftentimes it's because their core foundational blocks were

weak and poorly constructed. Not their fault, but it's the reality. No matter what they achieve, it's not right or good enough. It's not *integrated*. Look at, as another example, our political leaders. Raging narcissists. Why? Because they similarly are compensating for past wounds that get wrapped up into the present. And if you delve into their childhoods, you'll find the answer in bold letters.

When the time comes, I'll cry. That was my mantra, a mental heuristic I formed a long time ago. I had many mental shortcuts that steered my mind away from what I probably should have been paying attention to: my feelings and my hurt.

It was impossible for me to do so at the time because not only did I block any negative thing out, I also vowed to myself that nothing was a big deal to me. It was pure denial. I believed everyone had it worse than I did. There was no place or justification for my pain when so many others have it so much worse than I do.

I have many voices that speak to me. One of them is the one that says: "How dare I complain? How dare I speak ill of my experiences?" I battle guilt at every level imaginable. I feel guilt when anything great happens to me, especially if it's related to money or success. I feel guilt when I'm upset at a bad thing that happens to me. I feel so guilty when I even remotely find a reason to blame my past for how I feel in the present.

I never allow myself the opportunity to feel any sort of self-pity. The second any form of self-pity pops into my head, then another voice begins to scold me. "You ungrateful bastard!" That's what the voice says as it screams into my ear.

This other voice, the one that reminds me to continuously

feel guilt, always finds a way to remind me that others have it so much worse. As a result, I have always believed that everyone else has had it so much worse than me. So what if I was sexually abused? Others have it worse.

Empathizing with others was so easy for me. It's something I can do masterfully. Empathizing with myself, however—*that* I could not and can't do masterfully. Over time and a decade of therapy, I'm slightly better at it. It's difficult looking at my circumstances in my personal life with empathy. I just can't do it with my own stuff like I can with others. It was a reaction formation I developed, created, and mastered to ward off any unwanted feelings.

Over time, over hours upon hours in that little room, I began to break down that reaction formation and learn a new one. It wasn't easy.

I don't have wishes anymore, especially ones that take me backward in time. Wishing for the past to be different is foolish. Wishing to understand it is wise.

So here I am. The search for the "perfect" and that elusive "someday" has brought me to this point. The pursuit of my authentic self is a forever journey. I know now that there is no finish line. But there are certain mile markers to cherish, like the place I find myself now. It's the reason I found the need to reflect and write this book.

I think of myself as an ordinary person from a "life experience" standpoint. I look around and I see and hear of so many other people's lives that make my life seem silly and trivial. In fact, that consideration makes putting my stories on paper even sillier. *Who cares?* I think.

I suppose I have had some events happen to me that aren't the best. I have definitely had some challenges. But, as I tell Jeckel, although less frequently each time we meet: "It's no big deal. So many people have it worse." I'm great at minimizing everything and deflecting. Always pointing to people that have been dealt a much worse hand than I have.

Today, I believe my experiences have been "perfect."

Looking back I wouldn't trade a single one of my experiences for anything. I would never, in a million years, want to make that experience I had with my cousin go away. It was horrible, but it's part of who I am. I am so fortunate to have experienced that train ride from Iran.

I learned so much from all the moves. Nine different homes in the span of nine years! I cherish the fact that I had to repeatedly walk into school after school and start from scratch. All those events, coupled with an interesting family dynamic, made me who I am.

Now I like who I am.

Had I not had those events and situations, I'd never have met Jeckel. Had I not slipped into that dark abyss, had I not disconnected from reality, had I not flirted with the bottom, Andy and Brian would have never insisted with conviction that I get help. I wouldn't have discovered my true friends who stuck by me throughout all of this.

Today, my forty-five-year-old mind no longer believes that any event or circumstance is good or bad. They are just events in this journey. We don't know what we don't know. And we certainly don't have a crystal ball.

I feel that the childhood I had, including my parents and

my brother, was "perfect." I love them dearly and they love me. Sure, I wish we had communicated better, and sure, I wish my parents spoke better English. Sure, I wish they could have connected with me better and perhaps have authentically listened to me as child. But thank God it wasn't so. Who would I be then?

I consider myself very lucky. I feel blessed and wonder: "Why me? Why'd I get so lucky?"

I can't imagine who I'd be without those experiences.

I'm glad I got to meet the chemicals I used to pump through my body. Had the destruction not reached a tipping point, I am certain that I would still be the two discs on the yo-yo, up and down, and still not aware which way I was going.

I was blessed with the *perfect* amount of pain. Enough pain to make me mad and give me that edge and fight to help me overcome some challenges. Enough pain to force me to compensate, in the *short run,* for my insecurities. But not *too* much pain that would cripple me to a point of no return. Enough pain to send me deep into depression but just enough pain to make recovery possible.

As I was finishing these last few sentences in this book, I walked outside to take a break. On July 6, 2016, 11:24 p.m., I put on a song that has always made me feel good. Most of my memories with this song are alone. Headphones on, the song playing, and me lost in deep thought.

Tonight I look up. Stars everywhere. Some really bright and some not. These lights are many light years away. Some are thousands of light years away. I love looking up at stars. It helps to remind me of how small I am.

It's the same when I'm on a plane 30,000 feet up. Looking down, everything looks so small. I imagine me walking around, a little fly at best. Looking above at the stars and looking down at the earth from 30,000 feet are the same thing. Both are a symbol of my life and each is seen from the flip side of a telescope. This image fuels my sense of perspective. And serves as a reminder of how small I am.

I listen to the song "But Not Tonight" by Depeche Mode, a song that played in my ears as I was finishing this book and staring at the sky.

When I listen to this song now, it connects me to my seventeen- or eighteen-year-old version of myself. To this day, this song makes me feel something very powerful.

This song is maybe one of the most important songs I've ever loved. When I think about the lyrics, I find them curious. They're full of hope. Somehow, even in my darkest times, I guess I had an optimistic view and outlook of the future. I don't know how or why, but I'm lucky that I did. This songs describes so much how I view life.

> *Oh God, it's raining but I'm not complaining*
> *It's filling me up with new life*
> *The stars in the sky bring tears to my eyes*
> *They're lighting my way tonight*

It's so strange that I loved this song back then, as a lost teenager, before Jeckel and all the time I spent working on myself. The song described a feeling that I've been searching for.

And now, ironically, it's playing in my ears as I write the last few words of this book.

Today, to borrow a phrase from another Depeche Mode song, *I'm enjoying the silence.* Except I'm referring to the *silence in my head!*

I hope you enjoyed the ride as much as I have . . .

It's been perfect!

It was the perfect amount of pain . . .

Perfect pain.

Afterword

Several months after I finished writing this book, I sold my business: the one I took over from my dad and spent years and years building from one auto repair shop to seventeen.

The business was what I poured all of my ambitions and insecurities into. My financial success went a long way towards creating distance between who I was now and the scared little immigrant kid whose parents could barely make ends meet.

And then one day . . .I was done.

Over the course of a year, one of my friends was diagnosed with breast cancer, my wife was diagnosed with skin cancer, and another friend lost a child. It was like a "life alarm" went off. I started thinking about not settling with my "wants" or maybe, more importantly, I suddenly knew what I didn't want. But, I had this feeling that was so clear. The feeling was that it was time to reinvent myself.

Within months, I was in talks to sell my company. It might seem like a knee-jerk reaction. But it wasn't.

I have always felt trapped in the identity that I had now created. Being a community leader, businessman, and someone that people looked up to had me hooked. I liked success and the lifestyle it created, but deep down I knew I loved it for the wrong reasons. I was relentlessly trying to overcome being that immigrant poor kid and compensating for the needs that went unmet as child. The years of therapy clearly taught and highlighted that for me.

When these challenges happened, I simply woke up one day with a clear vision that life is too short for me to keep pursuing false idols. Time was running out for me to walk the talk . . .

If Jeckel taught me anything, it is that I was a very insecure little boy. Confused, connection-deprived, and lacking control. Money, popularity, success—all were medicines to ward those feelings off. But, Jeckel assured me, I would get stronger over time with therapy. The past will always be the past, but as I got healthier, I would be able to integrate my new tools with the realities of today and in turn, integrate this into who I am.

Well, who I really am is a free spirit. Who I am now doesn't *long* to impress everyone anymore. I only want to impress myself and make my friends and loved ones proud—that's it! A new scorecard.

It's that strength that Jeckel refers to that actually allowed me to even entertain exiting the business world. I'm aware that this is not an option for most. I'm blessed to have found myself in a situation to walk away. But, believe it or not, I feel like an under-achiever. I know have so much more potential to increase my wealth. I'm too young to stop, based on cultural norms. But I am completely at peace with my decision.

Before, I never would have been able to do something like this. I never saw a day that I could exit without disappointing my team. I loved the people who worked with and for me— they were like my family. Our sense of shared mission and loyalty was so strong. How dare I leave them? How dare I only think of myself?

Well, my years of therapy taught me, I could love them and simultaneously love myself. Those things didn't need to be tied up into one another. As much as I cared about my team, I knew that me doing everything just for them was also "off."

I was also certain that if I sold my business I'd slowly become irrelevant in the community. No more commercials, interviews, articles, or charity events associated with my identity as a successful businessman.

And yet, I knew I wanted a simpler life.

I believe the secret to life is *connection* and *love* . . .

The sooner I had the strength to walk my talk the sooner I was able to open myself up to love even more. Selling the business symbolized the culmination of creating a new identity, free of the need to climb the ladder that Persian culture and my own insecurities so badly demanded.

In fact, now I feel I can love my Persian culture more than I ever could before. I rebelled against it for all the wrong reasons. I rebelled against my parents and even my brother—whom I am also able to love even more now—for all the wrong reasons. I had to find a psychological "separation" from all this . . . that's the word Jeckel used to explain it . . .

In summary, I wanted a fresh start. Now that I'm an entirely differently constructed Parham, I wanted to live the next part of my life without a plan.

I'm excited to try living without a clear plan. I want to not fear wasting time. I want to *enjoy* wasting time and slowing it down. I want to be completely present at my daughters' activities without a cell phone distracting me. I want to embrace simple conversations with my loved ones.

I want to only seek genuine relationships, like the ones I was so blessed to have along the way, the ones that gave me hope to live. I want to take a whole lot of time to actually just waste the moment!

Many years ago, I told Jeckel I had to make a difference. Maybe a foundation to help young kids get therapy at a young age. Maybe something else. Whatever it is, it will be free from pressures to satisfy a need or to medicate an insecurity. Something that no one else could know about, and it would still be meaningful to me. Something that will only need to make me proud of myself.

Here's my start, in this book. Who can tell what the future holds?

Acknowledgments

I have so many to thank, but there are a few people that stand out who helped give me the strength and encouragement to write this book.

First and the foremost is my wife. What she endured wasn't fair and that makes her my hero. It was and is unbelievable how she truly believed in me. That faith that she held deep, over time, would prove to be the single most impactful factor that helped me cross a tipping point that I needed. I will forever be grateful for the sacrifices, support, and unconditional love that she provided me.

Second, is none other than Dr. Jeckel. I don't know why I was so lucky to find him. But somehow I did. I can't imagine I'd be here today had I not met him and had his guidance for almost a third of my life. Doctors do what they do for a variety of reasons. Money, power, fulfillment, etc. In his case, I'm certain of the reason he does this and it's this very reason that I am here today to tell the story.

Last and certainly not least . . . my editor, Kelsey. I was so lucky to find her. She was amazing in not only providing me great advice but also relentless encouragement. Her quiet confidence and her subtle ability to push me was powerful. I know I couldn't have done this without her . . .

About the Author

Parham Parastaran is an Iranian American who moved to America suddenly during the Iranian Revolution when he was nine. He is a graduate of the University of Illinois, and successfully owned and operated a chain of tire and auto stores until their sale in 2017. He is now a community leader and a philanthropist, and has begun working on a new tech venture. He and his wife, Jennifer, have three daughters and live in Champaign, Illinois.